# SOMETIMES YOU HAVE TO LOSE TO WIN

*How to Conquer Adversity and Fulfill Your Destiny...*

## Lionel L. Nowell III

outskirts
press

# Acknowledgements

This book is dedicated to my amazing wife, and preeminent partner, Denise. You are my best friend, motivate me to seek new challenges, and make everything we accomplish together possible. I am forever grateful that you are in my life, and will always love you.

To my daughters Tiffany and Michelle, sons Justin and Jared, and all of my adoring grandchildren, my sincere desire is that this book will inspire you to conquer adversity, live your dreams, and fulfill the destiny God has for your life.

Chad Strader and Lisa DiGirolamo-Conklin, I truly appreciated your in-depth reviews as I was writing this book. Your comments, suggestions, and insights were invaluable; thank you.

To all of the unknown authors whose stories and quotes appear throughout the book, thank you for sharing.

I also want to acknowledge my family and friends who provided me with encouragement, and unwavering support, as I was writing this book.

Finally, thank you to all of my colleagues, business associates, and the numerous people I have met along my journey that have inspired my life in ways big and small.

*Sometimes You Have to Lose to Win* is a testimonial to all of you.

# Table of Contents

# Prologue

Before a Diamond Achieves Its Brilliancy and Prismatic Colors, It Has to Withstand Extreme Temperatures and Intense Pressure…

As a consequence of an irreproachable provocation, "If you are so smart why haven't you written a book?" that my oldest son inquisitively posed to me, I was compelled—perhaps coerced might be a more appropriate way to describe it—to write my first book, *You Are Better Than Your Best*.

Consequently, in my unabated desire to demonstrate to my son, and quite frankly more saliently myself, that I was capable of compiling a narrative of thoughtful expressions and perceptions others might benefit from, I embraced the naïve challenge of composing my first book.

The obvious next question might be, which one of your precocious children persuaded you to pen your second book? You will be relieved to know that this book was not precipitated by any of my immediate family members.

Instead, I gathered the impetus to formulate *Sometimes You Have to Lose to Win* from a multitude of people that I have encountered who regrettably allowed despondency and apprehension to steal their joy, destroy their confidence, and commandeer their vision of a brighter future.

There is a pervasive misperception in our society that affluent people do not have problems, and smart people do not make mistakes.

In fact, many of you have become disillusioned with the false belief that if you are on the "right path" to being successful, nothing bad will ever happen to you, and you won't experience difficulties, or have sorrow in your life.

The reality is, many of the people that you perceive as being successful and happy have overcome anguish, poverty, and personal tragedies to arrive at the point where they are in their life.

A good friend of mine once told me, "You see the brightest stars when the sky is the darkest." Using that metaphor as a correlation, sometimes you need impediments and complications to bring out the best in you.

There will undoubtedly be instances in your life when you are in dire straits, or have a feeling of deep distress caused by a loss, disappointment, or other misfortune.

Accordingly, the most predominant characteristics necessary to achieve sustainable contentment are to be relentless in all of your pursuits, and learn from your shortcomings as well as your triumphs.

I would even go so far as to say you should endeavor to learn more from your so-called losses than you do from your inconsequential wins.

Believe it or not I have made a multitude of blunders in my life, and faced arduous situations. Nonetheless, through all of my trials and tribulations I learned that you have to let the strenuous times refine you, not define you.

What you perceive as a setback is often an opportunity for monumental, impactful knowledge to manifest itself in your life.

The truth is, sometimes you have to relinquish what you think you want so you can obtain what you actually need, and rightfully deserve.

*Sometimes You Have to Lose to Win* acknowledges the premise that everything happens for a reason, and you would not be the person you are today if you had not encountered the onerous events in your past.

Hence, to live your dreams and fulfill your destiny, you cannot allow your past, or current disappointments, to be justification for why you cannot do better, and be better.

Alternatively, acknowledge the bygone exasperating situations that occurred and view every event that seeks to obstruct, or hinder, your progression as a learning experience that is preparing you for an exalted future.

Most, if not all, of you at one time or another have encountered situations and circumstances where you felt defeated, overcome by anxiety, and at a loss for how to prudently precede forward.

As a result, you disparage yourselves, rehash your deficiencies, and embrace your negative feelings, trying to make sense of why terrible things only seem to happen to you, and not other people.

The fact of the matter is every adult person at some point in his or her life has confronted a situation, which at that specific moment seemed to be debilitating.

We all have had an occurrence where we said something akin to, "I lost, I am so embarrassed, there is nothing else left for me to do, it just was not meant to be, I am a failure."

While at that particular moment the complication you encountered might have been humiliating, frustrating, and even literally and figuratively painful, you cannot wallow in your misery and allow yesterday's sorrow and regrets to overshadow today's dreams, and engender you to settle for less than you unequivocally deserve.

Have faith, and trust that if you put forth the appropriate effort, and maintain the prerequisite attitude and perspective, immense accomplishments are forthcoming, and something phenomenal is going to manifest itself in your life.

Oftentimes, there are occurrences in your life when you know precisely what you need to modify to enhance your chances for obtaining an awesome outcome.

Yet, you constantly fabricate a rationale to justify why you cannot do this, that, or the other.

Consequently, provocative circumstances arise that literally compel you to institute a change, which you otherwise would not make.

I readily admit that neither you nor I can always fully comprehend, or articulate, why indubitable situations happen to us.

Nonetheless, despite your setbacks or perceived lack of success, you have to stay vigilant and keep progressing forward.

Everyone has a divine purpose in life, and a destiny to fulfill.

The ultimate question that you have to answer is, will you be persistent and attain the extraordinary life that is preconceived for you?

Circumstances are not always perfect, and people who wait for all of the conditions to be quintessential before they take action, forego the process of doing something that is required to actualize their goals and objectives.

You need to have the mentality that you do not care if something has not been done before; you are going to do it anyway. You are not concerned if no one will go with you; you will go by yourself. And, if you do not get encouragement from your family or friends, you will encourage yourself.

It is how you respond to the challenges you come up against that will ultimately determine who you really are, and what you will become.

Michael Jordan, who is arguably the greatest basketball player that ever played the game, was quoted as saying, "I've missed more than 9,000 shots in my career. I've lost almost 300 games. 26 times I've been trusted to take the game winning shot and missed. I've failed over and over and over again in my life. And that is why I succeed."

Who a person really is, and how resilient they are, is revealed not in good times, but in times when there is controversy, difficulty, or problems in their life.

Accordingly, sometimes it takes losing for you to know what is required to win.

In this book I dispense some pensive guidance, and divulge a few life-changing paradigms, to help you conquer adversity and fulfill your destiny.

The prevalent theme that you will encounter throughout this book is based on the premise that you have to stop being distressed, dejected, and disheartened.

You need to reflect the confidence that you merit, and have a God-given entitlement to a joyful, prosperous, and victorious life.

Unquestionably you have the capacity, and capability, to eradicate all of the deterrents that are preventing you from living the wholesome life you desire, and so richly deserve.

From the beginning to the end of this book you will discover acronyms, short stories, metaphors, personal experiences, and humor to help you comprehend, retain, and implement the advice I am articulating.

Therefore, I am optimistic that some of the anecdotes illustrated in this book will resonate with you, and parallel some of your past, current, or future experiences.

To be totally transparent, I must confess that I did not write this book with the goal of liberating everyone, because I realize that is an unrealistic goal, which is out of my control.

Based on unscientific research, approximately thirty percent of the people who read this book are not going to modify anything of consequence to enhance their life.

Another thirty percent will read the book, conjecture they already know everything I impart, and seek every rationale or explanation to predispose why what I am expressing does not make sense or apply to them.

Finally, there is the group of people who will read the book and at least attempt to implement some of the attributes I articulate into their life. These are the individuals I am seeking to enthrall.

I am extremely excited about what the future holds for you, and believe that if you are truly committed to being better than your best, and are not willing to accept less than you deserve, there is sagacity and knowledge dispersed throughout this book that will amplify your life spiritually, intellectually, and emotionally.

Life is meant to be challenging, rewarding, satisfying, and meaningful, not just tolerated.

Get prepared to transmogrify your perspective as we embark on an amazing pilgrimage that will show you "How to Conquer Adversity and Fulfill Your Destiny," because "Sometimes You Have to Lose to Win."

Lionel L. Nowell III

# Start From Where You Are

Ask Not How Far Must I Walk, Instead Say I Will Walk as Far as Is Needed…

Indecisiveness, procrastination, complacency, and trepidation are but a few of the onerous impediments that avert people from attaining the goals and objectives they aspire to achieve.

How often have you heard someone say the following?

- "I am going to start exercising as soon as I get in good physical shape."

- "There is no need for me to put forth any effort because nothing ever turns out the way I want it to."

- "The moment I start to feel happy, something terrible always happens."

- "I do not like trying something new unless I know I will be good at it."

- "I am never doing that again. History repeats itself, and if it was bad the last time, it will always be bad."

The aforementioned assertions are merely a representation of the excuses, and irrational protestations, you conjure up to justify why you have not set in motion the actions required to metamorphose your current circumstances.

The truth of the matter is, nothing changes until you take the proverbial first step that is necessary to start you on the journey to a monumental transformation.

Time and time again, people endeavor to convince themselves that if they continue their current course of action, without making any significant alterations, somehow things will magically be different.

Assuredly, not initiating substantive changes, and waiting, wishing, and wailing about where you are currently in your life, will not set you on a pathway to where you should be in your life.

I also encourage you not to spend time agonizing that you are not totally prepared before you begin to make a change.

As Baptist minister, activist, humanitarian, and leader in the African-American civil-rights movement, Dr. Martin Luther King Jr. articulated, "Faith is taking the first step even when you don't see the whole staircase."

It is through your journey that God makes you stronger. Therefore, instead of proliferating your mind with arbitrary constraints suggesting why you cannot accomplish what you desire, have faith and the belief that you can conquer any obstacles placed in your path.

To be victorious in any aspect of your life, you have to commence from where you are and initiate incontrovertible modifications to get to where you want to be.

Do not keep waiting for the perfect moment. Take the moment and make it perfect.

I fully comprehend, and acknowledge, there may be demoralizing circumstances in your past that contributed to the apprehension you retain today. The key is not to let your past dictate your future.

Throughout my professional career, I have encountered individuals who despondently attribute their infelicitous position in life solely to the fact that they have been disadvantaged, and other people who have attained or accomplished more were merely lucky or privileged.

One of the first steps to overcoming the obstacles hindering your opulent future is realizing that you cannot allow your life to be dictated by other people.

You are ultimately responsible for what you achieve or do not achieve in your life. Hence, you cannot concede, or relinquish, your God-given power to someone else.

Whenever you find yourself doubting how high you can ascend, how successful you can be, or whether you deserve to be happy, remember your past accomplishments, the trials and tribulations you vanquished, and all the trepidation you have already overcome.

In the words of A.A. Milne, author of *Winnie-the-Pooh*, "You are braver than you believe, stronger than you seem, and smarter than you think."

As I have become more sagacious, I now comprehend that a few people succeed because they are destined to, but most people succeed because they are determined to.

Consequently, to enhance your current predicament you have to put your faith in God, and eradicate all of the excuses you have developed for why you cannot achieve your goals and objectives. Your motto should be, "Why not me?"

Why can't you obtain a higher-paying job, start your own business, be healthy, lose weight, break an addicting habit, learn something new, or be loved and love someone in return?

You are in control of your destiny, so do not idly sit back and expect other people, be it your family members, friends, boss, coach, mentor, etc., to do things for you that you are not willing to do for yourself.

"Your crown has already been bought and paid for. All you have to do is put it on your head." (African-American novelist, essayist, playwright, poet, and social critic James Baldwin)

This quote resonates with me for three reasons. First, the words signify that every single person that came before you paved the way for your greatness.

Consequently, you have an obligation to become the absolute best you can be, so you can continue paving the way for future generations.

Second, the quote is a reminder that you already have, or will have access to, everything you need to achieve your destiny. All you have to do is recognize it, and believe it.

Third, this quote advocates that you should not accept less than you deserve, and settle for where you are and what you have, or you will never ascend to where you are meant to be.

The principal impediment preventing you from being a better you … is you. So start from where you are and make the prerequisite alterations to propel you to your rightful position in life.

Let me share a personal story that illustrates the point I am making.

When I was about fifteen years into my professional career, and employed as Director of Financial Services at the Pizza Hut corporate offices in Wichita, Kansas, I vividly remember receiving my annual performance appraisal.

The reason this occurrence resonates with me is because in my performance appraisal discussion, I was told by my manager that he and the company appreciated my hard work and dedication, but in his personal opinion he did not believe I had what it took to be a vice-president, let alone be considered in the future for other senior executive roles in the organization.

My manager concluded our discussion by saying, although it was almost certain that I would never get promoted beyond my current position, I should be happy knowing that provided I performed at an average level I would be able to maintain a comfortable standard of living for my family.

While I obviously perceived my manager's assessment as being unfounded, and very subjective, it was nevertheless a wake-up call.

Being confronted, at the age of thirty-five, with the notion that I was not going to advance beyond my current position was paramount to losing everything I had aspired for in my career.

As I reflected on the conversation with my manager, I initially had doubts about my skills and abilities, and pondered whether I was capable of being an influential senior executive.

Simultaneously I was also galvanized, and the thought of hitting the proverbial glass ceiling aroused me from my complacency.

Ironically, that performance appraisal discussion turned out to be one of the most transformational events that occurred in my professional life.

.

It would have been easy for me to resign myself to the idea that other people deemed I had peaked in my career, and achieved my full potential.

However, deep down in my soul I fathomed I was thoroughly capable of accomplishing more and progressing further in my professional career. What other people saw as the end, I envisioned as my new beginning.

Furthermore, throughout my life having someone tell me what I could not do inspired me to prove him or her wrong.

From my perspective it was my destiny to become a senior executive at a Fortune 500 company, and if I were not going to be afforded the opportunity to do it at this particular company, I would fulfill my dreams somewhere else.

A quote from the highly acclaimed poet, author, and civil-rights activist Maya Angelou sums up my feelings at that particular moment: "We may encounter many defeats, but we must not be defeated."

It was at this salient juncture in my life that I began to fully comprehend that much of what you achieve, or do not achieve, in your life is predicated on the choices you make.

I also learned through this single experience the importance of not listening to cynics and naysayers, and not allowing other people's perceptions of what you are, or are not, capable of attaining define you.

More importantly, you cannot succumb to the misperception that someone else's opinion is more critical to your long-term success and happiness than your personal view, or belief in yourself.

In the aftermath of that performance review, my wife and I sat down and had a heartfelt conversation about our long-term goals and objectives. Harmoniously, we were in unanimous agreement that a dramatic career change was necessary.

To assist me in cultivating an action plan for my reinvigorated future, I sought advice from my mentors, spoke with a few career consultants, and reaffirmed my commitment to achieving success in corporate America.

The process I initiated was intense and emphatic. Over the course of the next few months I revamped my resume, and engaged with a selected group of executive search firms to let them know that I would be interested in pursuing a career change, provided it was for the right opportunity.

I also attended career fairs, linked up with my college placement office, and leveraged relationships I had developed in my prior roles to apprise people of my desire to seek a new opportunity.

Along the way I spoke with numerous recruiters and human resources professionals, which led to a vast array of telephonic and in-person interviews.

The insights that I obtained from the various initiatives prodded me to reassess my objectives, and culminated in me making a career change, which ultimately was the impetus that propelled me to greater success and bigger accomplishments.

Nine months after having the aforementioned conversation with my manager, I resigned from my finance role at Pizza Hut to pursue a new opportunity with The Pillsbury Company in Minneapolis, Minnesota, hundreds of miles away from family and friends.

Making this career change was not easy, and there were innumerable reasons to accept the prognostication that I might be better off accepting the fate my manager had laid out for me.

The truth is I was comfortable in my role, was earning a decent salary, and had to weigh the impact of relocating my young family.

I also had colleagues reiterate to me over and over again how big of a risk I was taking.

Mind you, I fully comprehended I was taking a calculated career risk, because I accepted a lateral position at The Pillsbury Company with a verbal promise that if I excelled in my assignments, I would have the opportunity to be promoted to a vice-president role within a year or less.

Yet, despite the perceived risks, deep within my soul I also knew accepting the fate that other people had laid out for me would definitely not impel me to the achievements I was destined to accomplish in my life.

Relegating my past, and embarking on a new future, was necessary if I was going to provide myself the utmost opportunity to attain my dreams, and fulfill my ambitions.

Commencing a new role with a company that did not put constraints on how far, and how fast, I could progress in my career was invigorating.

It fueled my determination, and motivated me to put forth the extra time and effort required to be better than my best.

As I ascended the corporate ladder I also mastered the following skills, which might serve as a catalyst to help you excel in your career.

### Skills to help you excel in your career:

- Unless you are being asked to do something illegal, immoral, or unethical, be wholeheartedly dedicated to excelling in all of your endeavors.

- Be cognizant of what is strategically important to your company, and fully comprehend how the role you are assigned aligns with the overall objectives of the company.

- Stay informed about current events and news that impacts the business sector where you work. Subscribe to the Wall Street Journal, leverage social-media, read trade journals, watch news programs on television, etc.

- Learn the rules of the game, especially the unwritten rules. Once you comprehend what is required to enhance your odds for success, you will be able to strategize and develop an appropriate action plan.

- Never surprise the person you report to. Bad news does not get better with time. Therefore, always ensure you keep everyone apprised of potential issues or complications.

- Develop mutually beneficial social and professional networks. The more time and effort you put into growing and nurturing your connections to other people the more successful you will likely be.

- Get constructive criticism on your performance, listen intently, and ask innumerable questions.

- Act professionally and maintain a positive perspective. Strive to make your manager successful, while avoiding negative actions, denunciation, and aberrant behavior.

- Be assiduous, but challenge others in a positive, intelligent, and diplomatic manner.

- Seek opportunities to be supportive and cooperative with your colleagues. Cultivate relationships and be a superlative team player.

- Serve as a mentor to new employees and junior people in the organization.

- Volunteer for new projects. Solicit opportunities to acquire additional knowledge and new skills.

- Engage in professional organizations and be a positive representative of the company.

While being exceptional in your job is extremely important, I have come to appreciate that coupling an ebullient work ethic with the attributes I articulated above derives prodigious results.

Fast-forward eighteen years from the date of my taking that new opportunity at The Pillsbury Company: I retired from PepsiCo, Inc., as Senior Vice President and Treasurer.

Along with the success I achieved at PepsiCo I had a very accomplished professional career, which included senior executive roles with The Pillsbury Company and RJR Nabisco.

Even more rewarding is the fact that I was able to leverage the finance, strategy, leadership, and overall business management skills, which I garnered from the various senior executive roles, to be elected to serve on the board of directors for several prominent Fortune 500 companies, including American Electric Power, Bank of America Corporation, Darden Restaurants Inc., and Reynolds American Inc.

Life has a fascinating way of working things out.

If I had not been informed that my finance career at Pizza Hut was effectively over, I might have been compelled to remain at Pizza Hut and continued in my current role. And, I can only surmise how differently my life might have turned out.

12

What is even more interesting, and what many of you may not know is, when I was employed at Pizza Hut it was owned by PepsiCo.

In 1997, after I had left the company, Pizza Hut was spun off from PepsiCo, along with Taco Bell and KFC, into a new company named Tricon Global Restaurants, which later became known as Yum! Brands, Inc.

Ironically, Pizza Hut, the company that at one point in my youthful career suggested I would never get promoted, was formerly a division of PepsiCo, the company where I achieved my most significant career success.

Understandably, some people will conclude that I am an anomaly, overachieved, or was merely lucky. My perspective, however, is quite the opposite.

I believe by not letting someone else's perception become my reality, I received what I rightfully deserved.

In hindsight, Pizza Hut served the purpose that it was intended for, which was to impel me to fulfill my personal destiny.

I tell this story not to boast of my accomplishments, but to provide a glimmer of what is possible in your life if you start from where you are, work extremely hard, believe in yourself, and leverage your God-given abilities.

From that single event it became crystal clear to me that "Sometimes You Have to Lose to Win."

In fact, what some people perceived as losing was actually a life-changing opportunity, which provided the impetus for me to reinvigorate my career.

The important message that I want you to take away from my personal experience is, do not accept the exaggerated story of your demise. Believe immensely more in yourself than you do in other people when they label you a loser, or foreshadow negative outcomes in your life.

When you encounter an obstacle or get emotionally knocked down, pick yourself up, learn from your minor setback, and energetically move toward the grandiose rewards that are meant for you.

While it is true that everything that happens in your life may not be in your control, make absolutely sure you take unmitigated advantage of the things you can control, and catapult yourself toward your destiny.

Resigning yourself to a life that you do not relish, and allowing other people to define who you are and what you will become, is inauspicious. It also leads to a despondent, unfulfilled existence.

Stop making excuses, and quit waiting on someone else to do for you what you need to do for yourself.

When circumstances in life go against you—and trust me, everyone I know has faced challenges and obstacles—you can either let them define you, or let them refine you.

A friend of mine (to be respectful we will call her Deena) had what looked to be the perfect life. Deena was an attractive woman who had three beautiful children, a husband who was a lawyer, and they lived in a mini-mansion with a housekeeper who attended to their every need.

As a result of their palatial lifestyle, they were viewed as being the pillar of success in their community.

However, beneath the pristine exterior Deena projected to the outside world, sadness lurked. Deena's husband worked excessively and they had a very unfulfilled marriage.

And, to make matters worse, her husband made Deena feel as if all of their marriage issues were her fault, which destroyed Deena's self-esteem.

After years of going to counseling and attempting to make her marriage work for the sake of their children, Deena came to realize she was fighting a futile battle, and developed the courage to divorce her husband.

The divorce was contentious, and in the end Deena felt as if she had lost everything, including her opulent lifestyle, her image in the community, and her self-worth.

Deena spent the next few years going through various stages of grief, despair, anger, and sadness. Her life became stagnant, and Deena blamed every unpleasant thing that happened on her ex-husband.

Deena practically started every conversation with, "I am messed up because of my former husband," and Deena then proceeded to tell anyone who would listen how terrible her ex-husband was, and how dreadful her marriage had been.

One afternoon Deena was having lunch with one of her best friends, and she started commiserating about all of the horrible events that had transpired in her life.

Believe me, all of the people close to Deena were sympathetic of her turbulent prior life and attempted to be supportive, but having heard the story for the umpteenth time her friend finally said in a calm voice, "Deena, I understand you had a tumultuous marriage, but how long are you going to keep making yourself a victim?

Starting today you have to decide that you are going to move forward, and not keep looking backward."

Deena's friend recalls that initially she was not comfortable being so blunt and sharing her observations, because she did not want to minimize the traumatic experiences Deena had encountered.

However, after years of watching Deena regress and not move forward in a positive way with her life, she also felt compelled as a friend to help Deena help herself.

Clinging to the past, telling her sorrowful story, and striving to get other people to pity her kept Deena affixed to her suffering, and prevented her from healing.

Virtually everyone I know has encountered a demoralizing experience of some kind or another. People go through a divorce, suffer bankruptcy, have an unexpected death of a family member, lose their job, sustain health issues, etc.

Yet, individuals who understand that they have a divine purpose are resilient, and do not let the past define their life, or be an impediment to their magnificent future.

Ultimately there comes a point in your life when you have to shake off the burdens of your past, migrate away from all of the drama and the people in your life who are creating it, and focus on the positive, uplifting opportunities that reside in your future.

Life is too short to squander your time feeling despondent and melancholy. You deserve to be cheerful and contented.

As hard as it may be, when you are in a difficult situation try to remember that falling down is a part of life, but getting back up is living.

When a disappointing or disturbing event occurs, you have three choices: you can let it define you, let it destroy you, or let it strengthen you.

In essence, a setback is merely a setup for you to experience significant and substantial rewards going forward. Thus, each and every new day presents an opportunity for you to initiate an enhanced beginning.

To be perfectly clear, I am not being ingenuous and suggesting you can, or should, completely overlook your past—quite the contrary.

Unequivocally, in a number of instances there are indelible experiences you can garner from your past that will benefit your future.

The key to moving forward in a definitive manner is not to allow your past to overshadow your future, and prevent you from pursuing the life you desire and so rightfully deserve.

Circumstances do not always change immediately, but with time and patience you will begin to see the conclusive outcomes you covet and strived for.

The great news in this particular instance is that after reflecting on the conversation with her friend, Deena sought counseling to help her eradicate the resentment that she felt toward her former husband.

Deena came to understand, and appreciate, that recanting her past suffering was not beneficial, and encapsulated her in a life she did not want or deserve.

"Better by far you should forget and smile than you should remember and be sad." (Christina Rossetti, English poet)

Today Deena's life is substantially different than the one she relinquished. Deena is remarried to a wonderful man named Myron, and happier than she has ever been.

Now when Deena meets up with her friends the conversation is all about how fantastic she is doing, and the next exotic vacation that she and Myron are embarking on.

Subsequently, Deena has developed a positive attitude, and learned the self-actualization that comes from not letting her past experiences overshadow her exhilarating future.

Being in an exasperating marriage, and going through a traumatic divorce, was undoubtedly a devastating loss for Deena, but regaining a positive sense of her self-worth, and getting married to her soul mate, was a life-changing win.

Every person I know who has achieved their goal or desired outcome has failed, or had a life-changing experience, at some stage in their life.

The consistent advice I receive when I speak to these individuals is that to overcome any adversity, when you get knocked down you cannot stay down. Pick yourself up, brush yourself off, learn from your past, and build an awe-some future.

There is an inspirational quote (author unknown) that says, "Pain makes you stronger, fear makes you braver, and heartbreak makes you wiser. So thank the past for a better future."

While some may debate the merits of this particular message, there is no denying that past experiences can be instrumental in formulating a brighter future.

In Deena's case, she came to understand that to live the life she truly deserved, it was of utmost importance that she stop beating herself up and start building her life up.

Not surprisingly, what tends to scare some people the most is the uncertainty that accompanies making any type of change.

Moreover, I would venture to guess that a multitude of people reading this book have been stagnated by a prior traumatic experience, and you are contemplating whether or not you can implement a change that will embellish your life.

Perhaps the change you need to initiate is something small, or on the other hand it could be a life-changing decision.

Nonetheless, if there is a situation in your life that is averting you from pursuing your destiny, it is paramount for you to do something about it.

The pivotal question you have to ask yourself is why are you waiting to implement a change that could enhance your life and define your destiny?

Do you think your problems will magically disappear, and the circumstances will somehow automatically get better? Are you waiting for the perfect time to get started? Do you doubt your abilities? Or is it the fear of failure, and the thought of what other people might say or think about you?

Let me share a little secret with you. The situation will never be perfect, self-doubt has killed more dreams than failure ever will, and there will always be people who disagree with you, or try to discourage you from moving forward.

I learned a long time ago that fear is like a two-headed coin. On one side, fear can be beneficial because it prevents you from doing something imprudent that you might later regret.

On the other hand, fear can be devastating because it can prevent you from doing something monumental.

Regardless of your rationale for being reluctant to make a change, I want to encourage you to start from where you are today and take the necessary steps to get you to where you need to be tomorrow.

Maybe you have to begin with a minor change to build your confidence, but in any case you have to get started. Remember, no matter how insignificant it may seem the first step is the most important step you take, because if you do not take that first step your journey can never begin.

One of the best courses of action you can undertake to assist you in accomplishing your goals is to stay focused on your desired outcome.

Despite the impediments, keep progressing forward, and take the appropriate actions to get you where you need to be, rather than giving up too early, or worse yet never trying.

How many times have you made a New Year's resolution to lose weight, get organized, save money, learn a new language, finish reading a novel, etc.?

You start with the best of intentions, yet over time you do not follow through, and your resolutions become a thing of the past until it is time to make next year's resolution.

The distinct persona that I am compelling you to adopt is not a New Year's resolution, or a fad. It is a metamorphosis that will propel you to new heights, and supreme places, in your life.

I want to encourage you to live a superlative life, and wholeheartedly believe you are perfectly capable of achieving anything, and everything, you commit to accomplishing.

With that thought in mind, here are a few action steps you can implement to assist you in initiating the changes you desire in your life.

### *Action steps to initiate the changes you desire in your life:*

- Set aside 30 minutes each day to concentrate on what you are seeking to accomplish. Why is your goal or objective important to you, what are the benefits you will garner, and what obstacles might you encounter along the way?

- Formulate an action plan delineating the steps you need to take to consummate the success you want to achieve. Put your plan in writing. Be specific and break down the tasks you intend to pursue into simple, obtainable milestones.

- Create a timeline of your important activities or tasks to keep you motivated and focused. If unforeseen circumstances arise, do not get discouraged. Revise your plan, and the time line if you have to, but never give up on your ultimate goal.

- Do not let pride, your ego, or other people prevent you from realizing your objective(s). We all need positive reinforcement and support from time to time to help us actuate tasks we cannot do by ourselves. Therefore, seek mentors and advisors from various backgrounds and disciplines, so you can utilize their collective knowledge to help you navigate through the challenges encumbering your path to success.

There is an old saying (author unknown) that hypothesizes, "Today is the first day of the best days of your life."

I hearten you to embrace that philosophy, and starting today commence the process of manifesting the dreams you covet for your life.

While no one can do for you what you are unwilling to do for yourself, I unequivocally believe reading the forthcoming chapters in this book will instill in you the desire, courage, and passion that you need to step out on faith and fulfill your destiny.

Your best is yet to come. "Start From Where You Are" and activate the resourcefulness that will transform your life, but in doing so be sure to always follow "The Golden Rule."

23

# CHAPTER TWO

# The Golden Rule

"Do to Others as You Would Have Them Do to You." – Luke 6:31 (NIV)…

There once was a grandfather whose wife had passed away, so he went to live with his son, daughter-in-law, and their family. As the grandfather grew older, he began to slobber when he ate and occasionally spilled his food on the floor. Because of his eating habits the family placed him at a table in another room, and had him eat alone.

Once while he was eating, the grandfather dropped his glass bowl and broke it. His son scolded the grandfather, and henceforth got him a cheap wooden bowl to eat out of. The grandfather was so sad and unhappy.

One day not too long after that incident, the young grandson was working with wood. "What are you doing?" his mom and dad asked. "I'm making a wooden bowl," he said, "for when you two get old and must eat alone."

The son and daughter-in-law were devastated and instantly realized they had been inconsiderate, and were mistreating the grandfather.

Without any hesitation they replaced the grandfather's wooden bowl with a glass one, allowed him to eat with the family, and thereafter decided to keep quiet when he spilled his food.

This story was adapted from the Grimm brothers' "The Old Man and His Grandson" (1812). While there are various versions of this short tale, I think its underlying message resonates the true meaning of the golden rule, and enables us to ascertain how we might feel if the way we treated others was literally imposed on us.

The story also serves as a mnemonic that your affinity vis-à-vis others can have a profound impact on your future. Stop for a moment and contemplate if there is a symbolical figure like the grandfather whom you have ignored or mistreated, and what will be the implications to your future?

I grew up in an area west of downtown Columbus, Ohio, that is officially named Franklinton. Albeit to lifetime residents, my neighborhood was more commonly referred to as "The Bottoms."

Technically, the reason this area was nicknamed The Bottoms is because geographically Franklinton lies below the Scioto and Olentangy rivers' water level, and a floodwall is required to protect the area from an inundation of overflowing water from the two rivers.

However, a more veiled rationale for the nomenclature stemmed from the fact that most of the people living in Franklinton were low-income families who were at the "bottom" of the socioeconomic ladder.

I relished my childhood growing up in The Bottoms because everyone who resided there was part of my extended family.

Considering only a few of the houses in our neighborhood possessed air-conditioning, on hot summer nights the adults would gather outside on their porch, or on a neighbor's porch, while us kids engaged in lighthearted games in the yard, or rode our bicycles up and down the street.

What the people in our tight-knit community lacked in monetary status was more than offset by how proud they were of the non-material possessions they had accumulated, and the mutual respect they maintained for each other.

All of the families who lived in the vicinity of my house knew each other personally, and at an early age I was taught to treat everyone with respect, and convey to all of our neighbors the same deference that I would extend to my own parents.

As a result, I reverently referred to my neighbors as "Mr. and Mrs. So-and-So," and responded "yes" or "no, sir," and "yes" or "no, ma'am," whenever I addressed my elders.

Similarly, our neighbors treated me like I was one of their own children and did not hesitate to hand out praise, and punishment, when it was warranted.

While adhering to the Golden Rule sounds like a relatively simple concept, many people I know neglect to comprehend how their actions toward one another can establish and sustain, or destroy and diminish, meaningful relationships.

Staying faithful to the core values that I procured growing up in my small nurturing community has served me immensely throughout my life, and I have maintained to this day the practice of treating everyone I meet with respect and deference.

Regardless of whether it is the Chairman/CEO of a Fortune 500 company, or the waiter/waitress at a restaurant, I endeavor to exhibit to everyone the same decorum and thoughtfulness.

A colleague of mine conveyed the following story to me, which reinforces the point I am attempting to make about engaging with people in the same manner in which you would want to be treated.

During a student's second month of college, one of the professors gave the class a pop quiz. Being very conscientious one student breezed through the questions, until he read the last one: "What is the first name of the custodian who works in the building where this class is being held?"

Surely this was some kind of joke. The student had seen the custodian several times going about his tasks around the building. The custodian was a relatively tall man, grey-haired, and looked to be in his late 50s, but why would he even contemplate wanting to, or needing to, know his name?

The student handed in his paper, leaving the last question blank. Just before class ended, another student asked the professor if the last question would count toward the quiz grade.

"Absolutely," said the professor. "In your life you will meet many people from all walks of life. All of them are significant. They deserve your attention and care, even if all you do is smile and say hello."

The young student got all of the questions on the quiz correct except the last one.

Needless to say, he never has forgotten that lesson. He also learned the custodian's name was Anthony, and made it a point to introduce himself and say hello.

To further accentuate this sage advice, allow me to recap a personal experience that still resonates with me.

When I was a Senior Vice President at PepsiCo, I made an effort to stop at the security gate each morning and acknowledge the security guard as I proceeded into our office complex.

The security guard's name was Jay, and he would respond with a polite hello in return, and occasionally we would spend a few minutes casually talking about his family, how his favorite sports team was doing, or commiserating about the day's weather.

Regardless of how congested my day might be, I always took the opportunity to say hello, because I enjoyed my interactions with Jay, and simultaneously I wanted Jay to know I valued and appreciated him.

A contingent of my colleagues deemed it peculiar that I stopped every single day and took the time to talk to "the security guard."

The truth is, most of my peers viewed Jay as somewhat of an invisible man: he was there, but was not someone they needed to be concerned with, or squander their valuable time on.

While my colleagues' obsession over my treatment of Jay was a tad annoying, I have come to understand that you cannot be more concerned about what other people think about you than how you think of yourself.

Quite frankly, my acknowledging Jay, and treating him with deference, was a genuine gesture reflecting the values that were indoctrinated in me as I was growing up.

Hence, I remained resilient and ignored the fallacious comments.

One snowy evening I was driving home from work and got a flat tire. I contemplated calling the American Automobile Association (AAA), but I inherently knew, considering the horrendous weather, they were busy with more pressing problems, and it would take them quite a long time to respond.

I pulled my vehicle over to the side of the road, got out, and began the arduous task of extracting my flat tire so I could replace it with the spare tire from my trunk.

As I proceeded to change the flat tire a multitude of vehicles kept streaming by, splashing wet snow all over me, and as a consequence I became extremely wet, frigid, and tired.

After I had been at this pursuit for what seemed like hours, but actually was only about fifteen or twenty minutes, a vehicle pulled up behind me. A gentleman jumps out and says, "Hello, Mr. Nowell, I was driving home and went by you, but when I looked in the rearview mirror and saw it was you, I turned around at the next exit and came back."

That gentleman was Jay, the security guard whom I spoke with each morning. Admittedly Jay may have stopped in any instance, but one would be naïve to construe the informal relationship Jay and I had established did not play a small role in him coming to my assistance.

Incontrovertibly, I was truly appreciative that Jay aided me in fixing my flat tire, because what had begun as a bad experience ultimately culminated into a beneficial outcome.

Jay's altruism also reinforced my contention that if you treat people with mutual respect, and signify they matter, individuals will go out of their way to reciprocate the faith you have shown in them.

Through this escapade, it became apparent to me that some of the mishaps and defeats we encounter are of our own choosing.

Numerous people emotionlessly passed me by on that cold, snowy evening. Therefore, I am convinced the relationship that I had established with Jay was unequivocally the deciding factor in his decision to stop and provide assistance.

The lesson to be extracted from this personal experience is that you have to take the time to build relationships with people. Everyone you encounter has a role—maybe diminutive, or perhaps prodigious—to play in fulfilling your destiny.

It does not cost you anything to smile and say hello to someone, but it may have significant value to the other person. And, while it should not be your sole motivation, being nice to someone could be beneficial to you at a critical juncture in your life.

The reality is many of you are so oblivious and self-absorbed in your own little world that you miss an abundance of positive occurrences that are going on all around you.

One of the most unparalleled illustrations I have come across that exemplify individuals going above and beyond to be a positive inspiration for others is the Warrior Games.

The Warrior Games is an annual sporting competition that features five U.S.A. teams comprised of approximately 200 wounded, ill, and injured service members and veterans representing the Army, Marine Corps, Navy, Air Force, and U.S. Special Operations.

Teams compete in sporting events including archery, cycling, shooting, swimming, track-and-field, wheelchair basketball, and volleyball in a Paralympics-style competition.

The Games are designed to introduce injured service members and veterans to Paralympics sports competition, and encourage them to stay physically active when they return to their local communities following the event.

When one of the athletes, who'd had his legs amputated due to a bomb-related injury he endured while serving our country, was asked why he participated in the Games, he stated that he was extremely motivated by others like him.

"While talking with others with similar injuries, I realized that I could do anything I want," he said, "and I wanted to be a motivation for others." He continued, "I saw these younger guys, twenty and twenty-one years old, that had suffered debilitating injuries, and I knew that I could help them and show them what I learned from my injury."

Despite having suffered a life-changing physical loss, this soldier's primary objective was how he could help others deal with their injuries. The passion exhibited by this American hero is a true testament of "The Golden Rule."

Your life will be more gratifying, and you will be much happier, if you adhere to "The Golden Rule" by demonstrating to others the same acts of kindness you want them to exhibit to you.

It is my belief that oftentimes you are not even aware of the unintentional consequences your behavior has on other people.

Allow me to share five attributes you can implement to assist you in becoming more cognizant of "The Golden Rule," while enhancing the positive impact you exert on other people.

***Attributes to assist you in becoming more cognizant of "The Golden Rule":***

- Listen, be attentive, and convey interest in what other people are saying. How many times have you been texting, consumed with your iPad, watching television, or just blatantly tuned someone out when they were speaking to you? Instead of consciously or unconsciously ignoring someone, take a moment to defer what you are doing, look the person in the eyes, and give them your undivided attention.

- Be mindful of your tone and choice of words when you speak to other people—talk to people, not down to them. Attempting to purposely intimidate, embarrass, or belittle someone only makes you appear insecure and immature. Alternatively, be aware of how what you say, and how you say it, might impact the other person.

- Say "thank you" or "job well done" to people who partake in activities that make your life easier. When my wife visits the grocery store, she always thanks the person who bags her groceries. Initially I thought my wife's action was a bit over the top, as the bagger was just doing his/her job. However, my wife rightfully reminded me that she was grateful for the assistance they provided. And, while it was a small gesture expressed by my wife, the baggers always smiled and said "thank you" in return, which reflected their appreciation for the nice acknowledgement.

- Be courteous and demonstrate respect to other people, even when they do not always deserve it. Getting cut off by another vehicle when you are encompassed in traffic can be annoying and frustrating. It also can decimate your entire day if you allow it to. Rather than getting vexed and allowing a person you do not even know, and probably will never see again, to ruin your day, give them a smile instead of giving them an obscene gesture.

- Assume positive intent. Everything that people say or do to you is not meant to be demeaning or hurtful. As opposed to assuming everything is meant for your detriment, take a step back and look at the situation from a different angle. What you perceive as an insult might actually be someone trying to help you grow, and be more successful. Oftentimes we overact to what people are saying and assume the worst. This is particularly true with e-mails and text messages, where you cannot see the person's facial expression or body language. The next time you read or hear something that does not seem right, assume it was meant to be constructive—at least until you can positively confirm otherwise.

While these five attributes seem very simplistic, I can assure you from my own personal experiences they work and will have a tangible impact, while imparting a favorable impression on people you encounter.

It is probably safe to assume that you know someone who believes their title, position, or social status entitles them to be rude, uncivil, and disrespectful to other people. Unfortunately, a person's self-absorbed behavior can lead to a nescient perspective of life.

To be successful in any aspect of your life you cannot allow your ego, self-importance, or arrogant behavior to persuade you into engaging with people in a manner that is indecorous.

Always strive to be extremely conscientious of what you say and how you conduct yourself. Negative thoughts and actions bring about negative results and consequences.

Successful people whom I affiliate with understand and appreciate the virtue of treating everyone they encounter with respect. They are also confident enough to internalize that kindness is a towering strength, not a critical weakness.

My great-grandmother often used the phrase "You catch more flies with honey than you do with vinegar," which basically means treating people nicely will get you a lot farther than disrespecting them.

Every person is valuable and important in God's eyes. Consequently, the next time you consider saying or doing something that might be hurtful, stop, take a deep breath, and ponder for a moment how you would feel if someone reacted to you in that manner.

Yes, at that particular juncture you may feel euphoric, but I assure you that feeling will be temporary, because how you treat someone else will eventually boomerang back to you.

Along with adhering to "The Golden Rule," another important skill that will serve you well is learning how to be a person that you love, respect, and admire.

I vividly remember a song by the late great Whitney Houston entitled the "Greatest Love of All." The words in that song encapsulates the point I am articulating. In the chorus of the song Whitney sings out, "Learning to love yourself. It is the greatest love of all."

Acknowledging how valuable you are, and learning to love yourself, is extremely important for your self-esteem, and will facilitate happiness in all facets of your life.

I have met a number of men and women in their late twenties and early thirties who are fixated on finding a wife or husband to fulfill their life.

What many of these individuals fail to comprehend is that to be happy with someone else, you first have to decipher how to be happy with yourself.

You cannot surmise that someone will unequivocally love and respect you if you do not love and respect yourself first. Your character and integrity send a clear gesticulation to other people regarding how they should interact with you.

Inevitably there are people who disrespect themselves by doing things that disparage their mental and moral qualities, to entice a boyfriend or girlfriend.

If you choose to indulge people in a certain way because you are afraid to upset them, or want to win them over, you are invariably going to modify your behavior to obtain a specific response from that person.

You will also dedicate more attention to providing them what they desire, rather than being concerned with how much of yourself you are compromising to achieve that objective.

As a result, you can find yourself becoming someone you do not recognize, or even like.

The truth is that when you derogate yourself, or allow other people to disrespect you, you are essentially reinforcing to others that it is okay to mistreat you and disregard your feelings.

It is imperative as you pursue your destiny that you ascertain how to love, and be happy with, yourself.

"Don't rely on someone else for your happiness and self-worth. Only you can be responsible for that." I believe this stupendous insight shared by Stacey Charter, cancer survivor, divorce survivor, attack survivor, and all-around positive person, is a fundamental lesson that we all can embody and benefit from.

Another aspect of being comfortable with yourself is not becoming frustrated, or envious, when you observe other people achieving success.

Do not become jealous when an associate gets a promotion. Nor should you get frustrated when a friend or family member gets married, inherits a large sum of money, buys a new house, takes an exotic vacation, or gives birth to a beautiful baby, etc. Instead, rejoice in other people's happiness.

Jollity, prosperity, and contentment are your destiny, and what God has designed for your life is unique and perfectly fitted for you. Accordingly, nothing anyone else achieves is averting treasures that are promised and intended for you.

Therefore, you should not feel constrained in celebrating other people's successes.

I proudly profess that my prayer for all of my family members and friends is that they flourish in every aspect of their lives.

Why, you might ask, do I feel that way? Because, my family and friends being blessed is validation that I too can attain the destiny designated for my life.

I assure you that when you seek opportunities to make another person happy or content, are a positive role model, and exhibit the persona other people relish being around, you will in turn attract extraordinary blessings.

Life is full of tremendous opportunities, and inexhaustible rewards, so as you embark on your wondrous journey, always abide by "The Golden Rule," and if you encounter an exacting situation or are not confident you can attain your goals, do not give up, "Get a Taller Ladder."

CHAPTER **THREE**

# Get a Taller Ladder

Instead of Rationalizing Why You Cannot Accomplish Something, Give Yourself Reasons for Why You Can...

I am a prodigious sports fan, and thoroughly enjoy watching, and reading, stories pertaining to the extensive preparation, and tribulations, winners endured on their way to achieving a championship.

A notable testament that reveals what it takes to be a preeminent champion is highlighted in the 1970 National Basketball Association (NBA) finals, where the New York Knicks were playing the Los Angeles Lakers to determine who would be crowned the NBA Champions.

Willis Reed was the captain, and starting center, for the New York Knicks. In game five of the NBA finals Willis Reed suffered a torn muscle in his right thigh, which prevented him from playing in game six, during which Wilt Chamberlain, the starting center for the Los Angeles Lakers, had 45 points and 27 rebounds propelling his team to a win.

At that particular juncture the two teams had battled back and forth, with each team having won three games in the seven-game series. The deciding game seven was played on the New York Knicks' home court at Madison Square Garden.

As the two teams warmed up prior to game seven, Willis Reed was not on the court with his teammates, and most people doubted that Willis Reed was going to play in a game that would ultimately decide the championship.

Many basketball experts had already conceded that without Willis Reed the New York Knicks would not be able to contain Wilt Chamberlain, and therefore would lose the final game of the series, and as a result the NBA Championship.

However, unbeknownst to the Los Angeles Lakers players and the New York Knicks fans, Willis Reed had other ideas.

Prior to the tipoff, Willis Reed put on his uniform, received painkilling injections to numb the tear in his leg, and hobbled down the tunnel and onto the court.

The New York Knicks fans were exuberant and began to scream and cheer profusely as they caught sight of the New York Knicks captain.

Simultaneously, the Los Angeles Lakers players were stunned with disbelief as they stopped warming up and stared at Willis Reed.

Willis Reed started game seven and scored the first two baskets for the New York Knicks before limping to the bench.

While Willis Reed only scored those two baskets, his presence inspired the New York Knicks to a 113–99 victory over the Los Angeles Lakers, consummating in the New York Knicks' first NBA Championship.

Although other people doubted that Willis Reed would even attempt to play in the deciding game of the NBA Championship, his assessment of the situation was completely different: "I didn't want to look at myself in the mirror twenty years later and say I wish I had tried to play."

It is possible that the New York Knicks may have ultimately won the game without Willis Reed. On the other hand, it is unquestionable that Willis Reed's courage, determination, and strength of character, not only miraculously changed the attitude of his teammates, but instilled apprehension into the Los Angeles Lakers players as well.

I admire Willis Reed—not only for his basketball talents, but because he embodied the heart of a champion. Nursing a severe thigh injury and being in excruciating pain, no one would have faulted Willis Reed if he had decided not to play in the basketball game.

Yet, rather than complaining and harping on his limitations, Willis Reed grasped the opportunity in front of him, hobbled onto the basketball court, and created one of the most memorable moments in the history of Madison Square Garden.

Think about how many times in your life you have been confronted with a challenge, nowhere close in magnitude to what Willis Reed faced.

Nevertheless, rather than pushing forward, you doubted your-self, or allowed an obstacle to deter your progress and accepted defeat.

The reality is, if you do not try you have already lost, and doubt has killed more dreams than failure ever will. If you accept the challenge, and put forth a noble effort, at the very least you provide yourself an opportunity to succeed.

Allow me to share a personal story that illustrates what I discovered about the significance of not doubting yourself.

A few years ago my wife and I purchased a second home. The layout of the house was exactly what we wanted, but the previous owners had a passion for the color orange, and they had proceeded to express that love by painting a few of the walls a bright tangerine orange.

Ergo, without any hesitation my wife and I readily agreed the orange walls were going to be the first thing we remediated.

I must confess that I do not consider myself to be an expert handyman, but painting a few walls appeared to be an easy enough task.

Therefore, in lieu of hiring a professional painter, the day after we closed on the house, I jumped out of bed, gathered my painting supplies, took out my ladder, and frantically went to work painting over those orange walls.

My painting project was proceeding splendidly until I reached the living room, which has a high vaulted ceiling. I tried standing on the top step of my twelve-foot ladder—which I do not recommend by the way—and stretched as far as I could. Despite all of my efforts, I still could not reach high enough to paint the apex of the living room wall.

Being determined to not be defeated, and desperately wanting to finish the now half-painted wall, I got a broom handle and taped my paintbrush to it, the intent being to extend my reach by leveraging the broom handle.

Teetering on the top step of the ladder, I stretched out with the paintbrush attached to the broom handle, and still could not reach the top of the wall.

At this point I was getting extremely frustrated, and contemplated why I had even begun the process of painting the walls in the first place.

I also pondered the annoyance of waiting until we could hire a professional painter to finish my now incomplete project.

Sensing my mental disposition, and being rightfully concerned that I might do some serious damage to myself and/or the wall, my wife said, "Why don't you go to Lowes, or Home Depot, and 'Get a Taller Ladder'?"

That was a poignant moment for me, and needless to say, I learned a few valuable lessons that day.

Rather than being thoughtful about how to solve the problem, I had allowed myself to devote a significant amount of time and energy commiserating about the challenges, and obstacles, placed in my path, as opposed to deriving an applicable solution.

Unlike Willis Reed, who kept his eye on the prize and made a conscious decision to do whatever he could to help his team win, I was preoccupied complaining about how tall the wall was, and fixated on what I could not do.

As I reflected on the situation, the height of the wall was not the problem; my reaction to dealing with the height of the wall was the problem.

Far too often you spend an inordinate amount of time bemoaning the impediments and difficulties you encounter, and forget that life's problems would not be called hurdles if there were not a way to get over them.

"Get a Taller Ladder" is a metaphor for how you need to stop complaining and doubting your abilities, and start accumulating the habits, skills, tools, or resources you need to be successful.

Maybe you need to commence an alternative way of thinking about the situation.

Perhaps it requires navigating through intricate details, when it would be easier to quit. Or, you may have to revise your strategy or business model to achieve the desired results.

The bottom line is, to be successful in any aspect of your life there will be instances when you have to avail yourself to innovative ideas and diverse ways of thinking.

At the same time, you need to be dedicated, perform the difficult tasks that other people are unwilling to do, and be distinctly focused on accomplishing your goals and objectives.

In this particular instance, I listened to my perceptive wife and proceeded to purchase a thirty-six-foot extension ladder. Thereafter, the task I had previously perceived as being monumental quickly became painlessly simple and trouble-free.

It is inevitable that as you go through life you will encounter complications, adversity, and so-called losses, but keep in mind it is not what happens to you that ultimately matters; what is most important is how you respond to what happens to you.

During my travels across the country, I have observed that a critical attribute that prevents people from overcoming impediments in their life, and thereby achieving their destiny, is not being self-aware.

When I talk about self-awareness in this context, I am referring to having the conscious knowledge of one's own character, feelings, motives, strengths, weaknesses, and desires.

To be victorious in any endeavor, you first need to understand the reality of what you are up against. Once you comprehend what is impeding your success, then, and only then, will you be able to strategize and develop an appropriate plan of attack.

Too often people spend more time denying the reality of their situation than they do assessing their circumstances, and developing a judicious response.

In the words of former world number-one tennis player Billie Jean King, "I think self-awareness is probably the most important thing toward being a champion."

With that thought in mind, how well do you know yourself, and comprehend your strengths, and your opportunity areas?

Being open, and blatantly honest, with yourself about the situation you are in, and what characteristics you personally need to acquire, change, or eliminate to enhance your chances for success, is vitally important.

In many instances, you spend too much of your precious time and energy making excuses about why you cannot achieve something, or how impossible the task at hand is, rather than focusing on identifying a viable solution to the circumstances or hindrances, which lay in your path.

To fulfill your dreams, and live out your destiny, you have to come to the realization that just because something is arduous does not mean it is impossible.

Muhammad Ali, the greatest heavyweight boxer of all time, and one of the most significant sports figures in history, had this to say about "impossible":

"Impossible is just a big word thrown around by small men who find it easier to live in the world they've been given than to explore the power they have to change it."

Let me be candid: being conservative, and wanting to have a safeguard or safety net, to protect you against possible hardship or adversity, is not necessarily a bad thing.

However, when you assume the task at hand is impossible, or become over-reliant on taking the easy path and do not push your boundaries, your apprehension can prevent you from developing the self-reliance and confidence you need to achieve your goals and objectives.

At some stage in your life, you probably went to a circus and gasped with excitement and amazement as the flying trapeze artists performed their aerial act, while showcasing strength, coordination, and flexibility.

What you may not appreciate is that most of these performers, who so gracefully swing on high bars high up in the air, start out wearing a safety harness, where a person on the ground controls the lines as they practice, and pulls up on the lines if the performer falls or ends up in a precarious situation.

Pulling on the lines suspends the performer in the air, and slowly letting go of the lines brings the performer safely to the ground.

Hence, when the performers are wearing the safety harness there are limited risks, and the performer can focus on learning the tasks at hand, rather than being consumed with the fear of falling.

Eventually, once a performer has mastered the aerial act and is more comfortable, the performer takes off the safety harness and relies on his or her own skills and abilities.

While using a safety harness when you are refining and mastering your skills is an acceptable practice, at some stage it is expected that the safety harness will no longer be required.

One of the principal reasons many of the people reading this book have not achieved the ultimate success, and happiness, you are seeking is because you are fearful that if you step out of your comfort zone, and vigorously pursue your dreams, something bad or unpleasant will happen.

And, rather than reaching a point where you can rely on your own skills and abilities, you have become overly reliant on the invisible safety harness provided by your spouse, parents, boss, or a friend, etc.

The excessive dependence, or reliance, on someone or something, always being there to protect or take care of you, diminishes your personal growth and development.

As a result, you never stretch your boundaries, try new and different things, or most importantly, develop your talents and capabilities to the point where you can continue to grow and thrive on your own.

Let me provide you with an example of how staying in a place, or situation, where you always feel safe or at ease, and without stress, can be detrimental.

When I was growing up, speaking in large public settings was petrifying for me. I felt intimidated standing up and talking in front of a throng of people, and attempted to avoid it at all cost.

Once when I was in high school, I was presenting to my class-mates and became so nervous that the words got caught up in my throat, and I began to cough uncontrollably every time I began to speak.

That single experience haunted me for a long time thereafter. When I graduated from high school and attended college, I purposely selected large lecture classes or technical courses where I would not be called on to speak, as a way to mask my anxiety of public speaking.

Inexorably, the apprehension of speaking in front of a large group carried over into my professional life. It got to the point where, early in my career, I would defer to my colleagues during business meetings, and spoke as little as possible.

Not speaking when I was in a large group kept me in my comfort zone, and without my fully comprehending the negative impact, not speaking up also became my safety harness.

My reluctance to speak in large group meetings was not an obvious issue in the early years of my career, since I was in entry-level roles where I rarely had to make a presentation.

However, as I progressed in my career, not speaking up in meetings, and thereby sharing my insights and point of view, ultimately became a detriment to my success.

It reached a phase where I purposely rarely engaged in large group discussions, even when I had direct knowledge of the subject matter, and had a sufficient amount to contribute.

In lieu of being self-aware and acknowledging I was nervous of speaking up in meetings, I rationalized my discomfort by convincing myself that participating in business meetings was not that pivotal.

I was adamant, and a bit naïve, in thinking that since my boss knew I produced high-quality work results, it did not matter whether or not I spoke up in meetings.

While this statement might be partly true, the actuality is my not being self-aware masked the reality of the situation. In all honesty, I was limiting my career options by not speaking up in public forums, and could not get myself to admit it.

Worse yet, instead of contemplating the benefits I could derive by speaking up and being fully engaged in the discussions, I devoted my brainpower to rationalizing why engaging in the conversations during meetings was not worth the effort.

Fortunately, a few of my peers who knew me well took notice of the fact that I rarely spoke up in large group meetings, and they began to inquire why I was quiet in these settings.

At that point, it did not take a genius to realize my demeanor in meetings was clearly having an unintended impact on my performance.

Overcoming my fright of public speaking was not something that I was going to easily eradicate, but I also knew that if I did not finally address the issue, it was going to be an impediment to obtaining the goals to which I aspired.

The support and assistance I received from one of my mentors helped me to acknowledge the gaps between how I naturally interacted in non-group settings, and how I needed to behave to be more effective in large group settings.

Endowed with that knowledge, I initiated a few tactics to help me slowly face my trepidation.

As a start, instead of feeling pressured to speak up throughout the entire meeting, I focused on one or two salient points that I was totally comfortable with, and coaxed myself to voice a comment, or question, related to those specific topics during the course of the meeting.

To ensure I would actively adhere to my development process, I often attempted to be one of the first persons to speak. Not only did taking this approach relieve my tension, it also ensured others would not expound on the comments I was prepared to make, leaving me with nothing to say.

As a way to further enhance this process, when I was getting myself prepared for a meeting, I would often practice speaking out loud in front of my bathroom mirror, so I could hear the tone and inflection of my voice, observe my facial expressions, and test out what I was going to express.

In essence, I ceased using my imaginary safety harness in private, which eventually allowed me to slowly become more comfortable, and confident, in public settings.

Also, to inspire myself to engage more, if the opportunity presented itself, I attempted to interact one-on-one with people in the room prior to the meeting starting, and would share a few insights that I thought were beneficial.

As a result, oftentimes during a presentation, the presenter would mention that preceding the meeting I had commented to him or her about a specific topic, which reflected to the entire group that I was engaged and making a contribution.

Over time, with a great deal of practice and coaxing from my mentors, I became less anxious about speaking up in large group settings. Although it was not a natural occurrence, I eventually improved at sharing my point of view, and became more relaxed in the process.

Operating outside your comfort zone, and learning to flex your style, is never easy, but with coaching and perseverance you can learn to adapt.

One of the first steps to becoming more self-aware is being cognizant of the behavior(s) you need to eradicate.

Once you acknowledge what you need to change, you can put an action plan in place to expand your horizon, flex your style, and develop an authentic and effective approach to alleviate the situation.

Just like the trapeze performers, who have to practice and learn how to perform without their safety harness, your adaptation of new skills will take time, effort, and determination.

Yet, you will be successful if you remain diligent, and believe that you can, and will, overcome your impediments.

When self-doubt sets in, realize that oftentimes it has very little to do with you not being capable, or lacking the ability to accomplish a particular task. The simple fact is that you have retreated into your comfort zone.

People naturally find solace in their comfort zone, because when you branch outside of your comfort zone uncertainty, indecision, and doubt populate your mind.

You start questioning yourself, asking, am I smart enough? Or how will it look if I am not capable or am unable to complete the task? What will people think of me if I am not articulate, or they do not like my ideas or suggestions?

As a result of all the self-doubt you conjure up in your head, you experience trepidation, feel insecure, and decide it is best to say or do nothing. Regrettably, you also miss a huge opportunity.

You cannot allow your fears to determine your fate.

Become self-aware and realize that to achieve your destiny you have to focus on attaining what you desire, and stop making excuses to rationalize why it is okay not to achieve your goals.

One of my biggest motivators, and the inspiration that keeps me encouraged and steadfast whenever I contemplate quitting or giving up, is the legendary Nelson Rolihlahla Mandela.

Among his numerous achievements was Nelson Mandela's being South Africa's first black president. Although, it is the path Nelson Mandela took to attain his legacy that is so compelling, and motivates me to never give up on fulfilling my destiny.

Earlier in his life, Nelson Mandela was an anti-apartheid revolutionary and politician who led a campaign against the apartheid government in South Africa.

As a result, Nelson Mandela was subsequently arrested, convicted of conspiracy to overthrow the government, and sentenced to life imprisonment.

While he was imprisoned Nelson Mandela became a leader among his fellow inmates, advocating for improved treatment, better food, and study privileges.

Nelson Mandela earned a bachelor of law degree through a correspondence course while he was in prison, and became a beacon of hope for the anti-apartheid resistance.

During his time in confinement Nelson Mandela also continued to build his reputation as a political leader, refusing to compromise his beliefs to gain freedom.

Upon his release from prison after serving twenty-seven years, Nelson Mandela led negotiations that resulted in the democracy in South Africa for which he had always fought.

It would have been natural, reasonable, and even forgivable for Nelson Mandela to give up and allow the twenty-seven years he spent in prison to destroy him, and erode his motivation and influence.

Nevertheless, in spite of everything he endured, Nelson Mandela prevailed against seemingly impossible odds, and through it all fulfilled his destiny.

Many of you complain when you are faced with a day, an hour, or a mere twenty-seven minutes of challenges and tribulation.

Yet, what I glean from Nelson Mandela's life is an undeniable belief that if he can spend twenty-seven years in prison, and emerge to become the first black president in the history of South Africa, the circumstances you experience cannot define you, the limitations you have to overcome cannot deter you, and the obstacles you encounter cannot derail you.

Although life can be challenging, onerous, exacting, and formidable, you ultimately have to decide how you are going to react to debilitating circumstances, and overcome your apprehension.

This choice is inexplicably yours. You can make excuses and allow the stumbling blocks placed in your path to inhibit you, or you can heed a quote from Nelson Mandela that says, "It always seems impossible until it's done."

If you want something bad enough, you will find a way to obtain it. If you do not want it bad enough you will come up with copious excuses as to why it is not important, or possible.

When all is said and done, the significant question you have to answer is: what is bigger, your faith or your obstacles?

My message to you is, when you are confronted with adversity, tribulations, and challenges in your life, do not accept defeat and give up, "Get a Taller Ladder" and keep "Moving Onward and Upward."

# CHAPTER FOUR

# Moving Onward and Upward

The Road Less Traveled Is Often Where You Reap the Greatest Benefits…

Being persistent and continuing to systematically proceed onward and upward, even when the odds are seemingly stacked against you, is imperative if you are going to conquer adversity and fulfill your destiny.

At some phase in your life you were in all likelihood introduced to *The Wonderful Wizard of Oz*, the children's novel written by L. Frank Baum. Originally published by the George M. Hill Company in 1900, it has since been reprinted numerous times, most often under the name *The Wizard of Oz*, which is the title of both the popular 1902 Broadway musical and the well-known 1939 film adaptation.

You may recall that in the story a powerful cyclone carries the main character, Dorothy, from her home in Kansas to the magical Land of Oz.

Desperate to return home, Dorothy meets a good witch who tells Dorothy to follow the yellow brick road to the Emerald City, where the almighty, great Wizard of Oz might be able to assist her in getting back to Kansas.

As Dorothy embarks on her trek to the Emerald City she encounters a host of different characters, and endures numerous challenges and obstacles; yet undeterred, Dorothy continues "Moving Onward and Upward" to her intended destination.

I will not indulge you with all the intriguing details of everything that ensues in the story, but it is safe to say nothing could impede Dorothy from reaching her intended destination.

Dorothy's persistence, coupled with her can-do attitude, invigorated her to take the prerequisite steps that eventually allowed Dorothy to return home.

There are numerous learning's that emanate from *The Wizard of Oz*; however, the message that resonates the most with me is, each and every one of us has within our embodiment the inherent ability to create our own path to success.

Everything you desire for your life is feasible as long as you remain passionate, refuse to compromise your principles, and do not allow anything to interfere, or deter, you from your ultimate destiny.

Similar to the resolve that Dorothy demonstrated in *The Wizard of Oz*, you need to be methodically focused and adamant that nothing, or no one, will preclude you from attaining your desired objectives.

How many times have you started out with the best of intentions and subsequently, for a multitude of different reasons, you abandon your dreams, plans, or goals?

To invigorate your chances for success, one of the biggest impediments that you will have to overcome is the negative thoughts you conjure up that encumber your path, and prevent you from reaching your destiny.

Many of you reading this book are invariably searching to find your equivalent of the yellow brick road that will lead you to answers, which you believe will unlock the secret to a happy, fulfilled life.

While searching for answers is admirable, time and time again people fail in their attempt to obtain what they desire and deserve—not because they do not know the path they need to travel, but due to the fact they get distracted, refuse to take necessary risks, and close their mind to new ideas and different perspectives.

It is human nature that you want, and expect, your life to be uncomplicated, and trouble-free. As a result, you seek to maintain a simplistic existence, and allow your past experiences, monetary status, age, race, gender, education, and an array of other variables that you encounter, to impair your vision of what is possible in your future.

Consequentially, you do not follow the mythical yellow brick road that would enthrall your life.

Being complacent, and accepting the status quo, will not eradicate the barriers that are impeding your success. You have to be adventurous, and expand your perspective, because as the subtitle to this chapter articulates, "The Road Less Traveled Is Often Where You Reap the Greatest Benefits."

To be victorious at anything you want to accomplish, you need to possess an unequivocal belief in yourself and make intelligent decisions today, which will form the habits and behavior that lead to the success you want to manifest in your future.

In lieu of settling for where you are currently in your life, dream bigger and expect better. Furthermore, I would advocate that if your dreams and aspirations do not scare you then they are not big enough.

To conquer adversity and fulfill your destiny you must dismiss the negative thoughts that are impeding your progression, and exude confidence, because just like Dorothy in *The Wizard of Oz*, everything you require to be successful is already inside of you, or will be provided to you as you proceed on your journey.

No one can depress you, no one can make you anxious, and no one can hurt your feelings, unless you allow them to do so.

To emphasize this point, a few years ago I was invited to speak at a company's senior manager training program. I was speaking on the virtues of being better than your best, and the necessary traits that are required for you to be successful in any aspect of your life.

During my question-and-answer session a gentleman in the audience, who identified himself as Shawn, made a comment pertaining to the benefits that he had derived by working hard, and overcoming obstacles in his life.

Almost immediately a young woman, whose name I later learned was Brenda, stood up and sarcastically said, "He does not know anything about overcoming obstacles because he is privileged."

A quiet hush immediately fell over the room as people first looked intensely at Brenda, then inquisitively at me to ascertain what my response would be.

To alleviate the tension that had permeated the room, and wanting to delve deeper into Brenda's comment and perspective, I respectfully inquired if she could elucidate why she felt Shawn was privileged?

Brenda proceeded to share her perception of how Shawn obviously came from a wealthy family, considering he had attended a private boarding school growing up and graduated from an Ivy League college.

Accordingly, from Brenda's standpoint, Shawn could not possibly know what overcoming obstacles truly entailed.

Brenda went on to comment about how she had grown up in a lower-income family, went to public schools all of her life, and took out student loans to attend college.

Brenda concluded that based on the facts, she personally knew what overcoming obstacles entailed. Consequently, Shawn was definitely privileged and she was not.

I viewed the exchange between Shawn and Brenda as a teaching moment, versus a shaming moment, so I paused for a minute to digest both of their comments before expressing a point of view.

I proceeded to share with the group that I personally did not know Shawn, and certainly could not attest or deny if he was someone who had lived a privileged life.

However, the reality of the situation was that although Shawn and Brenda had traveled different paths, they were arguably at the same stage in their career.

Both of these individuals had been promoted numerous times since joining the company, despite having vastly different experiences.

Furthermore, I theorized that given Brenda's fast ascension into the managerial ranks, others in her peer group who had not progressed as rapidly as she did might conclude that she was privileged.

I proceeded to convey my personal belief that Brenda was a victor, not a victim. Therefore, publicly crowning Shawn as being privileged, and thereby inadvertently suggesting she was not, unintentionally bestowed upon Shawn special rights or advantages he had not rightfully earned.

At the same time, Brenda was unconsciously devaluing herself, and conceding that she was not an equal peer of Shawn.

Although it is probably true that Brenda had to work twice or three times as hard as Shawn to get to this position in her life, I wanted to ensure Brenda was not going to let the premise that Shawn's life may have been easier prevent her from celebrating her accomplishments, and believing in herself.

Let me be crystal clear: I appreciate there are times when you want people to understand your plight, and acknowledge that they have received an advantage which was not accorded to you.

However, as I have grown older and wiser, I have come to understand that in most situations achieving success, despite the circumstances you had to overcome, is the best revenge, and a righteous reward.

Being successful conveys that notwithstanding your trials and tribulations, you beat the odds, kept "Moving onward and Upward," and came out on top.

In that same vein, I am also cognizant of the fact that life is not always fair, but I cannot express enough the pitfalls of allowing the experiences that you encountered in your past to decimate your future, or be justification for your not succeeding.

In this particular example, Brenda had a tremendous amount to be proud of, and her numerous achievements conveyed that she had invariably worked hard and excelled to be held in such high esteem by the organization.

As a high-potential leader in the company with a stellar future ahead of her, Brenda was undoubtedly "Moving Onward And Upward," and did not need to compare the path she had traveled in her life to someone else's.

Moreover, Brenda needed to fathom that you can never allow past experiences to cast a negative perspective on what you are capable of achieving.

To illustrate this point, let me share a story that I heard about an elephant and an elephant trainer.

When an elephant is a baby, the trainer places a very thick rope around the elephant's neck and attaches it to a stake firmly hammered into the ground to tether the elephant. The baby elephant tries several times to get free, but at that young age, it lacks the strength to do so.

After a year, the stake and the thick rope are still strong enough to keep a small elephant tethered, although it continues to try, unsuccessfully, to get free.

At this point, the elephant subconsciously believes that the rope will always be too strong, so the elephant gives up.

When it reaches adulthood, the elephant can still remember how, for a long time, it had wasted its energies trying to escape captivity.

Therefore, at this stage, the trainer can tether the adult elephant with a slender thread tied to a broom handle, and the elephant will make no attempt to escape to freedom.

The strong, powerful grown elephants are physically able to easily snap the rope and break free, yet because of what they encountered as a young baby elephant they become mentally tethered to the past, believe themselves to be helpless, and accept their fate.

Many of you go through life limiting your full potential, and not achieving your destiny, because you are tethered to what someone told you, or the hardships you experienced in your past.

As a result, you concede that you are not as good, or do not deserve as much as the next person, when in fact you are smart, capable, and talented enough to accomplish whatever you desire.

To paraphrase the last two lines from a poem by William Ernest Henley, "You are the master of your fate, the captain of your soul."

The value you place on yourself will have huge ramifications on how others perceive you. Ergo, it is imperative that you are steadfast in your belief that you are a child of the most-high God, and something awesome is going to happen to you, and for you.

Yes, there will undeniably be times when no matter how persistent you are, situations will not turn out exactly the way you intended.

Nonetheless, rather than giving up and going through life tethered to the past, you need to trust in God, because sometimes what you think you want is not what you need.

In lieu of settling for a sub-par existence, allow the struggles you encounter to strengthen you and propel you to do monumental things.

In the case of my story about Brenda and Shawn, I am pleased to share that Brenda exhibited deference and ventured up to me after the session. Brenda respectfully thanked me for helping her realize she needed to stop attributing unintended value to someone else, and be proud of her accomplishments.

Understandably, I was impressed with Brenda, and have subsequently mentored her and watched her career excel. And, without question, a large aspect of Brenda's success can be attributed to the fact that she has not allowed her past to be an impediment to her future.

Brenda focused on what she needed to do to enhance her life, and ran her own race—which means, Brenda held on to her dreams, kept steadily moving toward her goals, and did not allow anyone to deter her from her ultimate destiny.

Contemporaneous to allowing the hardships of yesterday to become the focal point of today, procrastination is another debilitating attribute that averts people from obtaining their goals.

At one point or another nearly everyone has been indecisive, or postponed doing something you know needs to be done.

You think about initiating the tasks that you aspire to accomplish, and you have the best of intentions, but for one reason or another you just never get started.

When you procrastinate, you also tend to replace the critically important tasks you need to finish with other endeavors you like to do, which often are more fun and provide instant gratification.

While all of us are susceptible to procrastination, the issue comes about when procrastination starts to become a habit, and you constantly devise all sorts of reasons and excuses to delay taking appropriate actions.

You tell yourself that you are not prepared, or that you will start tomorrow. Inevitably tomorrow—"a mystical place where unused potential and unfulfilled promises reside"— never comes, more time passes, and you continue to delay taking actions that could transform your life.

In reality, procrastination is a detracting impediment that prevents you from pursuing your destiny. It also undermines all of your positive attributes, and diminishes your creditability.

Moreover, what some people fail to comprehend is that indecision becomes a decision over time. The more you procrastinate, the more arduous it is to commence doing anything productive, and as a result you are more inclined to not take any action.

People who know me well will attest that I am adamant about setting priorities, and having a written plan outlining what you desire to accomplish in your life.

I am also unyielding in my belief that you need to be motivated, and have a sense of urgency coupled with preparation, to activate your action plan.

The fact of the matter is, you will be rewarded and remembered for what you have accomplished, not for what you are planning or thinking about accomplishing.

The good news is that with practice and focus you can change your disposition, and put an end to procrastination.

Commencing new thoughts and new beliefs, which lead to appropriate actions, will help you expunge the habit of putting off, or delaying, something that requires your immediate attention.

To eradicate procrastination, you first have to prioritize the tasks that will provide you with the greatest benefit, because when everything is important, nothing is important.

You also have to learn how to postpone distractions and be methodically focused on deriving the best outcome.

Here are a few recommendations to assist you in alleviating your habit of procrastinating.

### *Recommendations to alleviate procrastination:*

- Separate your action plan into a clear, concise, doable list of tasks you need to complete. A list of small achievable goals, with firm deadlines, helps to make the bigger objective more obtainable. Also, completing items on the list instills confidence, and demonstrates your goals are realistic.

- Cross something off of your to-do list every day, or at a minimum each week. If you are not making progress against your objectives, erase the list and start over. Maintaining a list that you are not adhering to is a waste of time and counterproductive.

- Associate with motivated, action-oriented people. Observing other people succeed and accomplish momentous undertakings should inspire you to pursue your own goals and aspirations. Also, do not hesitate to seek assistance from people who can provide knowledge and insights on how to solve a particular problem you are encountering.

- Have faith in yourself and remain meticulously focused on your end goal. Along the way, celebrate small successes, and reward yourself for being diligent and adhering to your plan.

- Develop a group of accountability partners who will help to ensure you are adhering to your goals and deadlines. Most importantly, hold yourself responsible, and stop making excuses about why you cannot accomplish your objective(s). Be realistic and honest about your progress, and make appropriate adjustments when they are required.

- Do not delay; take the appropriate steps to get started today. Ensure you begin working on projects well ahead of the due date. When you are under pressure or preoccupied with other competing tasks, you are not as effective.

- Take a break, or walk away from the situation for a moment when you become overwhelmed, or feel frustrated. Clearing your head and regaining a calm composure can help you get reinvigorated.

- Appreciate that you do not always have to be a perfectionist and nitpick every little detail. Simplify what you need to accomplish. The goal is to complete enough small tasks so that over time you have collectively completed a big task.

- When you achieve a major milestone that will augment your life acknowledge your success and praise yourself for what you have accomplished.

- Solicit and embrace change. Be motivated by the fact that each and every day you are learning more, and getting better in some beneficial way.

Adhering to the aforementioned attributes may not be easy, but it will help you to overcome being a procrastinator, and vastly improve your chances for attaining success.

Extremely impressive or awe-inspiring outcomes do not materialize without some degree of effort and struggle. And, when you glance back over your life you will unequivocally cherish the times when you faced adversity, and conquered the obstacles in your path.

Abraham Lincoln, the 16th president of the United States, is credited with saying, "The best way to predict the future is to create it."

Therefore, do not cower when you face challenges, or seek to take the easy path. Believe in yourself and your abilities, and you will astound yourself with what you can accomplish.

There is a fable (author unknown), which accentuates that life is a reflection of the effort you put into it.

A son and his father were walking on the mountains.

Suddenly, his son falls, hurts himself, and screams: "AAAhhhhhhhhhhh!"

To his surprise, the son hears the voice repeating, somewhere in the mountain, "AAAhhhhhhhhhhh!"

Curious, the son yells: "Who are you?"

The son receives the answer: "Who are you?"

And then the son screams to the mountain: "I admire you!"

The voice answers: "I admire you!"

Angered at the response, the son screams: "Coward!"

The son receives the answer: "Coward!"

The son looks to his father and asks: "What's going on?"

The father smiles and says: "My son, pay attention."

The father screams: "You are a champion!"

The voice answers: "You are a champion!"

The son is surprised, but does not understand.

Then the father explains, "People call this an ECHO, but really this is LIFE. It gives you back everything you say or do."

Your life is simply a reflection of your actions. If you want different results, make different choices. Likewise, if you want more success, improve your preparation and effort.

Each situation you encounter is preparing you for a bigger, better, and brighter future. Keep taking steps, even small steps, in the right direction and your diligence and persistence will deliver you a monumental outcome.

Regardless of the problems and difficulties in life that come your way, know in your heart that you are truly blessed, and will eventually be victorious in all of your endeavors.

Do not allow your past to overshadow your future. Your best days are ahead of you, so keep "Moving Onward and Upward," and always "Believe in Yourself."

CHAPTER **FIVE**

# Believe in Yourself

It Is Not What Happens to You That Ultimately Matters, What Is Most Important Is How You Respond to What Happens to You…

As I was conducting interviews with a myriad of people in preparation for writing this book, the major difference that I discerned between individuals who had overcome obstacles and attained success, and those who were less triumphant, was not their intelligence, affluence, or ancestry.

Albeit there is no denying each of the aforementioned attributes plays a role in some people's achievements, I would submit that the most prominent distinction between people who attain their goals and people who do not is the unwavering confidence, passion, and persistence successful people exhibit.

Successful people have an undeniable belief that they can overcome any impediment, and accomplish their objectives.

Accordingly, to realize your aim or purpose in life, you have to confront every problem, challenge, negotiation, or task with an exalted expectation that despite the odds you can, and will, prevail.

Your mindset cannot be relegated to contemplating *if* you are going to succeed. Instead your time, energy and efforts must be devoted to analyzing how you *will* rise above the challenges placed in your path, and outperform your competitors.

The ensuing poem (author unknown) denotes the importance of maintaining a positive way of thinking or feeling about someone or something.

It also encapsulates the dissimilarity between the mentalities of a winner as opposed to that of a perennial loser.

- The Winner is always part of the solution; the Loser is always part of the problem.

- The Winner always has an idea; the Loser always has an excuse.

- The Winner says, "Let me do it for you"; the Loser says, "That is not my job."

- The Winner sees an answer for every problem; the Loser sees a problem for every answer.

- The Winner says, "It may be difficult, but it is possible"; the Loser says, "It may be possible, but it is too difficult."

- When a Winner makes a mistake, he says, "I was wrong"; when a Loser makes a mistake, he says, "It was not my fault."

- A Winner makes commitments; a Loser makes promises.

- Winners have dreams; Losers have schemes.

- Winners say, "I must do something"; Losers say, "Something must be done."

- Winners are a part of the team; Losers are apart from the team.

- Winners see the gain; Losers see pain.

- Winners see possibilities; Losers see problems.

- Winners believe in win/win; Losers believe for them to win someone has to lose.

- Winners see the potential; Losers see the past.

- Winners are like a thermostat; Losers are like thermometers.

- Winners choose what they say; Losers say what they choose.

- Winners use hard arguments, but soft words; Losers use soft arguments, but hard words.

- Winners stand firm on values, but compromise on petty things; Losers stand firm on petty things, but compromise on values.

- Winners follow the philosophy of empathy, "Do not do to others what you do not want them to do to you"; Losers follow the philosophy, "Do it to others before they do it to you."

- Winners make things happen; Losers let things happen.

As you can surmise from your perusal of this poem, there is often a thin line between being a winner and being an enduring loser.

Therefore, maintaining steadfast confidence that you will succeed, and being persistent in all of your tasks, is essential to actuating your destiny.

As you pursue your goals it is also crucial that you do not become disillusioned, and expect other people to make predicaments effortless for you.

No one owes you anything.

While other people can provide succor, you are ultimately responsible for exerting the efforts that are necessary to actualize your ambitions.

Let me share an intriguing conversation that might help you put the significance of taking personal responsibility in perspective.

A couple of years ago, while attending a nonprofit organization's fundraising dinner, I was introduced to a gentleman named Karl, who was a mid-level executive for one of the companies sponsoring the dinner.

Subsequent to a bit of small talk with references to where we both went to college and our favorite sports teams, the conversation evolved into Karl commenting to me that he was not sure if the company where he currently worked was suitable for him.

Karl proceeded to say that he was contemplating pursuing opportunities outside of the company for his next role.

Being a bit intrigued by his openness, I inquired of Karl what specifically was his rationale for pondering a career change?

Karl went on to explain that his current manager, who was also his mentor, was about to retire. As a result, Karl was uncertain how he was perceived in the company, and what the implications of the impending changes would be for him.

As it turned out, I had previously met Angela, the senior executive of the department at the company where Karl worked.

Although our interactions were limited, it was perceptible to me that Angela was a staunch supporter of diversity and inclusion, and someone who took great pride in mentoring younger colleagues.

Without revealing to Karl that I knew Angela, I queried, "What about your manager's boss, is he or she a supporter and advocate of yours?"

Karl quickly acknowledged that he admired Angela and suspected she was a genuine supporter, but considering Angela's high-ranking position in the company, he was reluctant to approach her and foster a relationship.

Consider this for a moment: Karl, who I had just met that evening, was openly sharing his frustrations with me.

Yet, he was reluctant to metaphorically reach out to Angela, who was someone that could be extremely advantageous in helping him realize his career ambitions.

Unfortunately, this was not the first time I had observed an individual vocalize that they were hesitant, or resistant to interface with someone who could be an advocate for them.

I often hear defeatist explanations like, "I think he/she may be too busy to meet with me," "They are too senior in the organization to be bothered," "What would I say to them," or "How will he/she react to my asking to meet with them?"

My reply is invariably the same: "How do you know what response you will receive unless you ask?"

I learned a long time ago, if you make inquiries in the appropriate manner, you have better than a fifty-fifty chance of getting a positive response. Alternatively, if you do not ask, you have already predetermined the answer is "no."

As I have reiterated throughout the earlier chapters in this book, leveraging all of the resources you have at your disposal is paramount if you are going to be successful.

Following are a few tips, which might assist you in your endeavor to get introduced to people, that could be beneficial to your success.

***Tips to meet people who might be beneficial to your success:***

- Ask your boss, a colleague, or a friend who already knows the person you desire to meet if they will facilitate the introduction. The old saying "It is all in who you know" is completely true, especially when it comes to networking.

- When you first meet someone be a good listener, and do not pry into a person's personal life. Allow him or her the opportunity to share with you, confide in you, and provide you information. Listen more, talk less, and you will be seen as one of the best people to engage with on a recurring basis.

- Schedule a brief meeting to inquire more about the business, task, or project the person you are interested in meeting is working on. Do your homework beforehand so you have a grasp of what specific questions and comments are applicable and appropriate.

- Volunteer for an organization, activity, or undertaking that will provide a natural extension for you to interact with the person you want to meet. In the process, you will be doing a good deed, fostering a relationship, and learning more about this individual while they are concurrently getting to know you better.

- Leverage social media sources like LinkedIn to introduce yourself and network with people. Post news articles, or topics of interest, which might invoke a response from people you want to meet.

- When you attempt to meet new people, have some tolerance for uncertainty and rejection. Everyone you desire to meet may not instantaneously want to engage with you. Therefore, you may have to flex your style and try different techniques.

The point I am making here is that if your intent is sincere and you approach a person in a genuine manner, most people grasp the opportunity to talk about themselves, or the activities they are interested in and are proud of.

Your challenge is to "Believe in Yourself," step out of your comfort zone, and not allow your apprehension to deter you from achieving your goals and objectives.

As I thought more about believing in yourself, and overcoming the obstacles placed in your path, I was reminded of a story rhyme that I read a few years ago about a group of frogs.

The tale (author unknown) goes something like this.

Once upon a time there were a bunch of tiny frogs that arranged a climbing competition. The goal was to reach the top of a very high tower.

The day of the contest, a big crowd gathered around the tower to observe and cheer on the tiny frogs.

As the race began, no one in the crowd honestly believed that any of the tiny frogs would reach the top of the tower.

You heard statements shouted out from the crowd such as: "Oh, that is way too difficult!" "They will never make it to the top!" "Not a chance that they will succeed!" "The tower is too high!"

As the race proceeded the tiny frogs began collapsing one by one, except for a few frogs that kept climbing higher and higher.

The crowd continued to yell: "It is too difficult!" "None of you tiny frogs will make it!"

More of the tiny frogs got tired and gave up. However, one frog was not deterred and continued climbing higher, and higher, and higher.

This one little frog refused to quit and was determined to reach the top.

As time went on, all of the frogs had given up climbing the tower except for one tiny frog who, after a big effort, was the only frog who reached the top of the tower; he was the winner.

All of the other tiny frogs that had failed to reach the top naturally wanted to understand how this one frog managed to climb the high tower.

One of the other frogs approached the tiny frog that had been successful in climbing the tower, and asked how he had mustered the strength to succeed and reach the top of the tower?

Lo and behold, it turned out that the tiny frog that had reached the top of the tower, and thereby won the race, was deaf and could not hear the discouraging words that were being projected at him from the crowd below.

In lieu of being dissuaded by other people's perspectives of what was possible, the tiny frog believed in his abilities, and just focused on climbing to the top of the tower.

The moral of this story is that to be successful at anything you desire to accomplish, you have to be persistent, "Believe in Yourself," and never allow the negative inducements that you hear, see, or read to dictate your actions.

Invariably, instances will arise when your family, friends, colleagues, bosses, the media, etc., will attempt to plant seeds of doubt and make unflattering, non-motivating remarks to impede your success.

In those instances, it will be imperative for you to turn a deaf ear and not pay attention to other people's opinion when they tell you what is, or is not, possible.

If you listen to the naysayers and give up, or do not try, you will never know what you can accomplish.

While all of us have dealt with uncertainty, successful people believe in themselves and comprehend that if they are persistent in pursuing their goals, despite the challenges they encounter, they will ultimately prevail.

Allow me to share some characteristics you can implement in your life to help you activate the self-confidence that is imperative to "Believe in Yourself."

### *Characteristics to help you "Believe in Yourself":*

- Visualize yourself achieving your goal or dream. This approach is frequently utilized in sporting events. For example, soccer players attest that they gain extra confidence by visualizing the soccer ball going into the net before they take a penalty kick.

- Do not allow negative people to steal your joy just because they have lost theirs. It is easier for most people to be negative than positive, and natural for them to be critical versus supportive. Surround yourself with passionate people who will encourage and inspire you.

- Celebrate and be proud of your successes. Forget about what everyone else might think of you; chances are they are not thinking about you that often anyhow. Boost your confidence by remembering the good outcomes, as opposed to the bad outcomes.

- Develop and safeguard your belief system. Do not provide an opportunity for negative people to fill your heart and mind with uncertainty or non-inspirational content. Also, identify and prioritize your ethical values, and have clarity on what is important in your life.

- Be kind to yourself. Do not beat yourself up for making mistakes. You are more capable than you give yourself credit for. Create a positive narrative about your dreams and goals that only include the circumstances that matter. Be your own best friend, instead of being your own best enemy.

- Eliminate self-doubt, and do not live your life with fear or resentment. Never give up without a fight. If you are reluctant to try you have already lost, and are invariably foregoing an opportunity to embellish your life. Although it takes tremendous courage and energy to get out of your comfort zone and attempt something new and different, just do it. There is nothing to regret if you put forth the appropriate effort.

- Write down your goals and place them in an auspicious location, where you will see them every day. Constantly remind yourself of the jubilation you will experience when you accomplish your objective.

- Speak and act with confidence, even if you are not completely self-assured. Portraying self-confidence gives you greater control over your ability to influence the outcome of decisions.

A prominent aspect of believing in yourself hinges on you engendering a reason to be happy. Instead of viewing life with a negative perspective seek out positive occurrences in each and every day.

Many people put off their happiness; they think, "I will be happy when I get that new job, when I lose weight, when I am in a relationship, when I am making more money, when I become famous, etc."

You have to realize that happiness is a daily choice. Therefore, no matter what your situation, if you approach life with a positive attitude you enhance your chance to be successful.

Be a dreamer, a thinker, and a doer and turns your obstacles into opportunities.

Also, strive to run your own race, at your own pace. You cannot compare yourself to other people, because no two situations or circumstances are the same, and people's strengths and weaknesses are distinct.

The reality is, there are often times when your biggest weakness can become your greatest strength.

Take, for example, the story (author unknown) of a ten-year-old boy who decided to study judo, despite the fact that he had lost his left arm in a devastating car accident.

The boy began taking lessons with an old Japanese judo master and was doing well, so he could not understand why, after three months of training, the master had only taught him one move.

"Sensei," the boy finally said, "shouldn't I be learning more moves?"

"This is the only move you know, but this is the only move you will ever need to know," the sensei replied.

Not quite understanding, but believing in his teacher, the boy kept training.

Several months later, the sensei took the boy to his first judo tournament. Surprising himself, the boy easily won his first two matches.

The third match proved to be more difficult, but after some time, his opponent became impatient and charged; the boy deftly used his one move to win the match. Still amazed by his success, the boy was now in the finals.

This time, his opponent was bigger, stronger, and more experienced. For a while, the boy appeared to be overmatched.

Concerned that the boy might get hurt, the referee called a time-out. The referee was about to stop the match when the sensei intervened.

"No," the sensei insisted, "let him continue."

Soon after the match resumed, the boy's opponent made a critical mistake: he dropped his guard. Instantly, the boy used the one move he had learned to pin his opponent.

The boy had won the match and the tournament. He was the champion.

On the way home, the boy and his sensei reviewed every move in each and every match. Then the boy summoned the courage to ask what was really on his mind.

"Sensei, how did I win the tournament with only one move?"

"You won for two reasons," the sensei answered. "First, you have almost mastered one of the most difficult throws in all of judo. And second, the only known defense for that move is for your opponent to grip your left arm."

Thus, what the boy perceived as his biggest weakness had become his greatest strength.

Regrettably, you sometimes erroneously spend more time focusing on what you do not have, versus possessing the faith that what you do have is enough, or will be conferred to you.

As a result, when circumstances go against you, or situations do not turn out the way you planned, you stop believing in yourself and accept defeat.

What you neglect to realize in these instances is it is not what happens to you that ultimately matters; what is significantly more important is how you respond to what happens to you.

If situations in your life do not materialize exactly the way you intended, you need to have faith and persevere; there is another path that will deliver you the ultimate outcome you are destined to achieve.

You can see this faith and perseverance at work when someone loses an unfulfilling job and subsequently receives a higher-paying role they are passionate about, a prospective student gets rejected at one college and thereafter gets admitted to an Ivy League school, or when someone that you thought was indispensable walks out of your life, and your soul-mate enters your life.

While losing something that you thought you wanted never feels good, you have to acknowledge that sometimes one door has to close so something greater can be revealed to you.

A wonderful example of believing in your dreams, while maintaining your faith and perseverance, is embodied in one of my mentees, Chad.

Growing up, Chad worked in his family's auto-repair shop, and he always had an interest in someday owning and operating his own business.

Chad's absorption with being an entrepreneur intensified when he read the book, *Why Should White Guys Have All the Fun*, which was written by Reginald Lewis. The messages in the book further energized Chad, and he became enamored with starting his own private equity firm.

After graduating from college, where he majored in accounting to hone his financial skills, Chad obtained a financial analyst role at a Fortune 500 company.

While the job provided Chad with good remuneration and extensive finance experience, Chad was still obsessed with the dream of starting his own business.

Subsequently, Chad took a bold step, quit his full-time job, and went to work, without pay, as an intern for one of his mentors who had started a private equity firm.

Chad assumed that since he was working for one of his mentors, the transition would be straightforward.

However, after several months of working as an unpaid intern, Chad was unceremoniously terminated, primarily because he lacked the skills, knowledge, and business awareness required to be successful in the private equity world.

Being fired was arguably the most humbling moment in Chad's young professional career. Albeit, from that setback Chad learned never to take anything for granted.

The experience also reinforced that if Chad wanted to achieve his goal, of owning his own private equity firm, he would need to augment his finance skills, and learn everything he could about the private equity business.

Undeterred, Chad did not give up on his dream. Instead he took actions to enhance his finance skills by applying to, and being accepted at, The University of Chicago Booth School of Business.

When Chad arrived in Chicago to attend business school, he immediately sought to secure an internship with a private equity firm, with the intent of fully learning the business this time around.

Chad quickly realized he was not the only MBA student interested in an internship at a private equity firm. The competition was fierce.

Sometimes the best way to win is by playing a different game.

Accordingly, Chad concluded that as an alternative to applying for internships, where the odds were diminutive, he would apply for a full-time job instead.

Furthermore, Chad devised a plan to obtain the full-time job by bringing the private equity firms what they really desired: a business deal.

Chad started to source potential deals, and used an imaginary firm (Red Arts Capital) to get investment banks to liaise with him. After weeks spent shifting through tons of documents, sending thousands of e-mails, and making numerous phone calls, Chad discovered a potential business deal, and pitched it to a few private equity firms.

All of his efforts paid off when one of the firms agreed to hire Chad in exchange for him allowing their firm to pursue the prospective deal.

Although the business deal did not culminate into a transaction, the private equity firm kept its word and hired Chad. Chad went on to work forty-plus hours a week at the private equity firm, while also attending business school full-time.

Over the next two years, Chad mastered the intricacies of conducting business deals. Chad also assisted in the consummation of several business transactions, and built a great network within the finance community.

After graduating from business school, Chad was presented with the dilemma of continuing his career as a business associate at the private equity firm where he had been working, or pursuing his longtime goal of launching his own company. Chad chose the latter.

Although Chad endured numerous setbacks and had to overcome tremendous adversity, Chad believed in himself and achieved his dream of commencing his own private equity firm.

Today Chad is a partner/cofounder of Red Arts Capital. Ironically, Red Arts Capital is also the name of the imaginary firm that Chad conceived years ago, when he was attempting to secure his first business deal.

Chad's life has come full-circle, and emulating the path initiated by his hero, Reginald Lewis, Chad is well on his way to achieving all of the decorum that being a successful investor, entrepreneur, and business owner bestows.

Chad's story is a manifestation of a quote by author George Bernard Shaw: "People are always blaming circumstances for what they are. I don't believe in circumstances. The people who get ahead in this world are the people who get up and look for the circumstances they want, and if they can't find them, make them."

While situations may look dim, and do not always go the way you conceived or expected, everything happens for a reason, and you always need to reassess and reconsider all of the possible outcomes.

I want to conclude this chapter with a motivational message that someone sent to me a few years ago.

For all of the negative things you have to say to yourselves, God has a positive answer for it.

You say: "It's impossible."

God says: "What is impossible with man is possible with God." – Luke 18:27 (NIV)

You say: "I'm too tired."

God says: "Come to me, all who are weary and burdened, and I will give you rest." – Matthew 11:28 (NIV)

You say: "Nobody really loves me."

God says: "For God so loved the world that he gave his one and only Son, that whoever believes in him shall not perish but have eternal life." – John 3:16 (NIV)

You say: "I can't go on."

God says: "My grace is sufficient for you, for my power is made perfect in weakness." – II Corinthians 12:9 (NIV)

You say: "I can't figure things out."

God says: "Trust in the Lord with all your heart and lean not on your own understanding; in all your ways submit to him and he will direct your paths." – Proverbs 3:5–6 (NIV)

You say: "I can't do it."

God says: "I can do all this through him who gives me strength." – Philippians 4:13 (NIV)

You say: "I'm not able."

God says: "And God is able to bless you abundantly, so that in all things at all times, having all that you need, you will abound in every good work." – II Corinthians 9:8 (NIV)

You say: "It's not worth it."

God says: "And we know that God causes everything to work together for the good of those who love God and are called according to his purpose for them." – Romans 8:28 (NLT)

You say: "I can't forgive myself."

God says: "If we confess our sins, he is faithful and just to forgive us our sins, and to cleanse us from all unrighteousness." – I John 1:9 (KJV)

You say: "I can't manage."

God says: "And this same God who takes care of me will supply all your needs from his glorious riches, which have been given to us in Christ Jesus." – Philippians 4:19 (NLT)

You say: "I'm afraid."

God says: "For God has not given us a spirit of fear and timidity, but of power, love, and self-discipline." – II Timothy 1:7 (NLT)

You say: "I'm always worried and frustrated."

God says: "Give all your worries and cares to God, for he cares about you." – I Peter 5:7 (NLT)

You say: "I'm not smart enough."

God says: "It is because of him that you are in Christ Jesus, who has become for us wisdom from God—that is, our righteousness, holiness and redemption." – I Corinthians 1:30 (NIV)

You say: "I feel all alone."

God says: "Never will I leave you; never will I forsake you." – Hebrews 13:5 (NIV)

The connotation of the aforementioned messages is that what you see as obstacles in your life, God sees as opportunities. God is always there for you. All you have to do is put your trust in him and expect the unexpected.

The best is yet to come. Rather than surrendering and becoming discouraged when situations and circumstances do not go the way you intended, you have to stay positive, maintain your faith, and develop alternative plans, if necessary, to achieve your destiny.

Your path to success is predicated on the desire, determination, and dedication you place on obtaining your goals. "Believe in Yourself" and embrace life as you travel along the road to your destiny, but also remember, "If It Were Easy Everybody Would Do It."

# If It Were Easy Everybody Would Do It

A Comfort Zone Is a Beautiful Place, but Nothing Ever Grows There…

In all likelihood, over the course of your life, it has been reiterated to you over and over again that if you work hard enough, you can achieve all of your goals and aspirations.

In fact, this highly regarded advice has been bestowed on some of you so many times that the concept of working hard has become purposeless, and does not inculcate anything in you.

Not surprisingly, most of you sincerely believe that you are working hard, yet despite your unrelenting efforts, it does not seem as though you are making progress in life, or realizing your objectives.

The harsh reality is, like many people I have encountered, you in all probability have a misconception of what working hard truly entails.

Occasionally staying late at work to complete your normal responsibilities, studying to get good grades in school, taking care of your adolescent children, ensuring your household is neat and tidy, attending to personal obligations, etc., are all admirable traits.

But, the truth is, while your daily activities can seem onerous and at times burdensome, most of the endeavors you experience on a day-to-day basis are merely methodical, routine tasks, which are necessary for your livelihood and existence.

Working hard entails being extremely diligent, and putting forth an extraordinary effort that goes far above and beyond your typical undertakings.

Working hard also necessitates that you exceed expectations, and separate yourself from the masses by doing whatever it takes to accomplish your objectives.

The gist of the title of this chapter, "If It Were Easy Everybody Would Do It," signifies that working hard is not something that everybody can, or will, embrace.

Working hard is in essence a metaphor for being relentless, and requires that you have the passion, resolve, and aspiration to surpass what is typically expected or predicted.

To quote American statesman and retired four-star general in the Unites States Army Colin Powell, "A dream doesn't become reality through magic; it takes sweat, determination, and hard work."

If you surmise that you are working hard but not obtaining the results you covet, I would propose your prognosis is predicated on one of the following factors.

***Factors that impact your ability to obtain results when you surmise you are working hard:***

- You are not implicitly working as assiduously as you think, or as diligently as is necessary, to achieve your desired outcome. Oftentimes people tend to compare how hard they are working to someone else. In actuality, the notion of working hard is unique to each individual and cannot be selfsame. The extra effort you need to exert to achieve your goals is indubitably not equivalent to what is required for someone else to accomplish his or her objectives. To attain your desired results, you have to avoid comparisons, concentrate on what it takes for you to be successful, and be undeniably devoted to always putting forth an unparalleled effort. My youngest son is a medical student at Columbia University College of Physicians and Surgeons. One of the most important lessons he learned during his first year of medical school is that you always have to strive to be better than what you perceive as your best. "It takes what it takes" is my son's motto.

- You lack focus, or your efforts are centered on the wrong activities. Concentrating your time and energy on unimportant tasks will not derive the same benefits, or positive outcomes, as being fixated on situations that truly matter. What some people neglect to comprehend is that a critical component of deriving miraculous outcomes is focusing on the right tasks, at the appropriate time. To magnify your odds for success you have to measure your effectiveness by your results, not by your efforts. Prioritize your actions, and ensure that your mental and physical capacity is immersed in situations where you can acquire the greatest advantage.

- You start out fervently, with a lot of commitment, but thereafter lose your motivation, and subsequently do not endure long enough to secure the maximum benefits. In lieu of continuing to press toward your goals, you seek the path of least resistance, and when you encounter adversity you cease putting forth the appropriate exuberance that is required to obtain your desired outcome. The beginning of anything you attempt to do is always the hardest; success takes time so learning not to quit is paramount if you want to achieve the exemplary results you are seeking.

The way you react when you are comforted with problems and adversity can also elucidate whether or not you are truly working hard, or simply going through the motions.

As an example, when circumstances do not go your way, do you complain about life not being fair, and make excuses, or blame others, regarding why you did not achieve your goals?

Successful, hardworking people understand that rather than blaming others, and commiserating about everything that went wrong, they have to continue to pursue their essential course of action, and not capitulate.

If you are spending time complaining about your situation, rather than seeking ways to invigorate your situation, you are assuredly not working hard.

It is irrefutable that losers see working hard as a punishment, while winners embrace working hard, and prevail in spite of their perceived problems and obstacles, not in the absence of them.

Another important element that should parallel your being diligent, industrious, and zealous in your pursuits is the concept of working smart.

To attain your goals you have to be astute in solving problems, so you can employ the most strategic methods to attain what you desire, and ensure outcomes transpire in your favor.

Some people postulate that working hard and working smart are mutually exclusive.

Contrarily, my perspective is that working hard and working smart are intertwined. Hence, you need to actuate both to achieve your goals and objectives.

Here, for your perusal, are a few attributes you can implement to help you work smart, concurrent with working hard.

*Attributes that can help you work smart, concurrent with working hard:*

- Seek an expeditious, or uncomplicated way to accomplish your objectives. This does not imply that you should act illegally, expunge important details, or do something in a manner that makes the quality of your work less valuable, or incomplete. Streamline the process by first understanding what is required to accomplish your tasks, and then evaluate if all of the actions and steps are necessary.

- Leverage your network of friends, and your business connections, to assist you in developing your action plan, or to help you solve difficult problems. Do not be reluctant to ask for support, or utilize people who can lend a helping hand, should you require access to additional resources and/or information.

- Acknowledge and appreciate your strengths and weaknesses. When it is feasible, concentrate your focus and attention on the projects that match your strength, while delegating tasks that fall in your areas of weakness to someone else.

- Do not complicate the initiatives you are undertaking by attempting to complete a myriad of tasks all at once. Prioritize and manage your time. Commence by first completing the most important tasks that will have the greatest impact on whatever it is you are attempting to achieve.

- Analyze what needs to be accomplished and be open to acquiring new skills, or adapting to a different way of doing things, so that you can enhance your chances for success.

- Everyone makes mistakes; therefore, do not hesitate to admit when you have made an error. It is never beneficial to invest your time, and your resources, into a lost cause. Do what you can to make the best of the situation, understand what went wrong and why, and then move on. Albeit, you need to ensure the same mistake is not repeated in the future.

As you strive to achieve your destiny, it is undeniable that working hard, coupled with working smart, will be instrumental in determining your long-term success.

Accordingly, be conscientious in leveraging both your implacable effort, and your intellect, to your utmost advantage.

Simultaneously with working hard and working smart, being strong-willed and unrelenting in the pursuit of your goals, even when it appears all odds are against you, will always serve you better than vacating your goals, and whining about your predicament, when the going gets tough.

The concept of being strong-willed and unrelenting reminds me of a story (author unknown) I heard about a farmer and his donkey.

There once was a stubborn old donkey that was so ornery that even the farmer who owned it did not particularly like this donkey. The farmer owned a large property, and one day he heard in the distance the loud, distinctive "eye-ore, eye-ore" of the donkey.

The farmer wondered what the stupid donkey had done this time, so the farmer looked all over his property until at last he found the donkey at the bottom of an old abandoned well.

Exasperated, the farmer rang his neighbors and asked them each to bring a shovel. The farmer concluded there was no viable way to get the donkey out of the well, so he had decided it would be better to bury the donkey in the well.

All of the farmer's friends came over and together they started to shovel dirt into the well. At first, the donkey protested loudly, braying with all of his might, but after about 10 minutes, the donkey stopped bellowing.

The farmers kept shoveling. After a while one of the farmers decided to have a look into the well to see what had happened to the donkey. What he saw astonished him. Instead of being buried, the donkey would dodge the incoming dirt, standing on the ever-increasing mound.

Seeing how the donkey was reacting, the mission changed, and the farmers went from trying to bury the donkey to trying to save him, shoveling more and more dirt into the abandoned well until the donkey jumped out of the top, victorious.

Upon his release, the farmers all dropped their shovels and applauded the old stubborn beast with a newfound admiration.

The moral of the story is, there will be times in your life when you may feel like you are being dumped on, and there is no way out of your predicament.

Yet, the stubborn old donkey shows us that being tenacious, never giving up, and discovering a way to vanquish your challenges will foreshadow your victory.

Living your dreams and fulfilling your destiny will not be easy; "If It Were Easy Everybody Would Do It." But, consider this: the satisfaction, and pleasure you will derive when you ultimately attain your goals will far surpass any pessimistic situations you have to overcome.

To help you remain relentless and enthusiastic as you pursue your goals, here are a few actions you can incorporate into your life.

***Actions to help you remain relentless and enthusiastic as you pursue your goals:***

- Banish negative thinking from your mindset. Look for the positive side of every situation, and envisage a favorable conclusion. In lieu of seeing the glass as half empty, view it as being half full; in every set of circumstances there is always something to learn and benefit from.

- Spend time with individuals you love and respect. Sharing memorable experiences with people you are fond of will allow you to appreciate life more, and makes all the obstacles you have to overcome worthwhile. Also, knowing there are people who believe in you, and want nothing but the best for you, makes everything you accomplish more significant.

- Engage and interact with other motivated, exhilarating people. Negative, pessimistic people deplete your energy, and have a dubious impact on your attitude. Seek out people who are buoyant and confident about what they do. Those people will inspire you and make your life much more gratifying.

- When you feel physically or emotionally drained, or situations are not going your way, step back and take time to relax, reflect on the positive attributes, and get reenergized. When you venture back to the task at hand, you will be more invigorated and embrace your challenges with a fresh perspective.

- Seek out pragmatic feedback. Obtaining inspiration and encouragement from others will help you improve each and every step along the way. Even when you receive criticism, turn it into something positive and use it to get better. Also, when you receive compliments or plaudits, revel in it and let it stimulate you to do even more unprecedented things.

Along with working hard, working smart, and being strong-willed and unrelenting in the pursuit of your goals and aspirations, another important aspect of success and happiness that people often overlook, or fail to realize, is that life is about choices.

Bluntly speaking, the choices you make, or for that matter the choices you do not make, play a prominent role in determining what you will or will not achieve.

The disinclination to make a decision, or indecision, has often been passed off as merely having patience.

However, I would assert that indecision is the reluctance or inability to make up your mind, and decide a course of action, when you are wavering between two or more possible outcomes.

As a result, whether you realize it or not, indecision is similar to procrastination.

To the contrary, patience is having the ability or willingness to tolerate, or temporarily delay something, without getting annoyed, angry, or upset.

Hence, indecision and patience are undoubtedly not compatible.

Demonstrating the ability to make choices quickly, effectively, and confidently is a valued characteristic that can be instrumental in dictating your long-term success.

Some people have trouble forging choices owing to their fear of making a mistake, and being wrong. They are petrified of the potential consequences that might arise from settling on the wrong decision.

What these people fail to realize is, "In any moment of decision, the best thing you can do is the right thing. The worst thing you can do is nothing." (Theodore Roosevelt, 26th president of the United States)

Contemporaneously with the trepidation of being wrong, people deter making decisions because sometimes settling on the right choice can be arduous, or they do not believe the complex problem they are facing has a feasible solution.

The following story (author unknown) reflects the predicament you can find yourself in when you encounter a difficult or seemingly unviable decision.

Many years ago in a small village, a farmer had the misfortune of owing a large sum of money to the village moneylender.

The moneylender, who was old and cunning, fancied the farmer's beautiful daughter. So the moneylender proposed a bargain. The moneylender said he would forgo the farmer's debt if he could marry the farmer's daughter.

Both the farmer and his daughter were horrified by the proposal. Therefore, the cunning moneylender suggested that they let fate decide the matter.

The moneylender told the farmer and his daughter that he would put a black pebble, and a white pebble, into an empty moneybag. Then the daughter would have to pick one pebble from the bag.

If the daughter picked the black pebble, she would become the moneylender's wife, and her father's debt would be forgiven.

If the daughter picked the white pebble, she need not marry the moneylender, and her father's debt would be forgiven.

However, if the daughter refused to pick a pebble from the bag, her father would be thrown in jail.

The moneylender, the farmer, and the daughter were standing on a pebble-strewn path in the farmer's field. As they talked, the moneylender bent over to pick up two pebbles.

When the moneylender picked the pebbles up, the sharp-eyed daughter noticed that the moneylender had picked up two black pebbles and placed them into the moneybag.

The moneylender then asked the daughter to pick a pebble from the moneybag.

Now imagine that you were standing in the field. What would you have done if you were the daughter? If you had to advise the daughter, what would you have told her?

Careful analysis would engender three possibilities:

I.   The daughter could refuse to pick a pebble, whereby her father would be thrown in jail.

II.  The daughter could reveal that there were two black pebbles in the moneybag, exposing the moneylender as a cheat, which might result in the moneylender becoming so enraged that he reneges on his offer, thereby leaving her father in debt.

III.   The daughter could pick a black pebble, and sacrifice herself, in order to save her father from his debt and imprisonment.

Take a moment to contemplate the story. Your analysis might lead you to the conclusion that there is no viable solution to the complex dilemma.

Well, here is what the daughter did.

The daughter put her hand into the moneybag and drew out a pebble. Without looking at it, she fumbled and let it fall onto the pebble-strewn path, where it immediately became lost among all of the other pebbles.

"Oh, how clumsy of me," the daughter said. "But never mind, if you look into the moneybag for the one that is left, you will be able to tell which pebble I picked."

Since the remaining pebble is black, it must be assumed that she picked the white one. And, since the moneylender dared not admit his dishonesty, the daughter changed what seemed like an impossible situation into an extremely advantageous one.

I doubt you have ever faced a contentious decision that is even remotely comparable to what the daughter encountered.

Nonetheless, this story reinforces that when you are confronted with a seemingly impossible decision, you have to remain positive, be creative, and devise ways to turn the odds into your favor.

As the subtitle of this chapter states, "A Comfort Zone Is a Beautiful Place, but Nothing Ever Grows There." Inevitably there will be times in your life when you will be required to step out of your comfort zone, and make tough decisions.

Regrettably, when faced with an exasperating decision, a lot of people often wait until the outcome is decided by circumstances that are outside of their control.

As a result of waiting, you place the decision in someone else's dominion, rather than making an enterprising choice that could impact your destiny.

Deferring a decision, or worse yet, not making a decision, means you are capitulating your role in determining your future, and allowing other people to decide what you do, or do not, achieve.

Furthermore, indecision rarely, if ever, makes the situation better. Everything does not have a perfect ending, and putting things off just delays your ability to quickly take corrective action.

I am a big believer in controlling your own destiny, and concur with American orator William Jennings Bryan's assertion that "Destiny is not a matter of chance; it is a matter of choice. It is not a thing to be waited for, it is a thing to be achieved."

My advice when you are faced with a difficult decision is to consider all of your options, obtain appropriate advice, conduct additional research if necessary, but when you are done with all of these steps, make a prudent decision.

The quicker you act, the more alternatives you will likely have available to you. Leaving your decisions until the last minute, or over-thinking the situation, does not improve the outcome, and typically the options available to you dwindle significantly.

Similar to the daughter in the aforementioned story, to be successful in any endeavor, you have to take control of your destiny, comprehend what is impeding your success, and then strategize and develop an appropriate plan of attack.

As I mentioned earlier in this chapter, working hard, so that you can accomplish your dreams, was never meant to be easy. Hence, no matter what path in life you decide to pursue, to be successful you will on occasion have to make sagacious sacrifices.

Sacrifices can be worth it if they facilitate your achieving the outcomes you desire, or living the life you want, but the sacrifices you make should be purposeful and not endure forever.

For example, when playing the game of chess, certain chess pieces are strategically sacrificed to gain an advantage over the other player, which results in the player who made the sacrifice winning the game several moves later.

Accordingly, enduring appropriate sacrifices is paramount as you pursue your goals and dreams, because it places you in a position to obtain the more consequential reward that you ultimately desired.

Outlined are a few of the sacrifices you may have to endure to fulfill your destiny.

***Sacrifices you may have to endure to fulfill your destiny:***

- Free Time – The value of time is literally priceless; there are only twenty-four hours in the day, so you have to make every minute count. Hours spent watching television, playing video games, and doing other unproductive activities will need to be eradicated, so you can raise yourself up from the place you are now to the place you want to be.

- Social Life – Carousing and socializing with your friends will need to be curtailed. If you do not learn how to say "no," or forego an evening out so you can focus on your work or studies, you will eventually suffer and not be effective in obtaining your goals. Some people will not understand, and call you unbalanced for relinquishing your social life and working so hard. My counsel to you is to take a break to relax when you really need to, but understand that by deferring those temporary moments of satisfaction, you are a step closer to accomplishing your goals and aspirations.

- Sleep – Allocating the necessary time and energy into attaining your goals will deplete the hours you have available to sleep. Yes, getting the proper amount of rest is absolutely important. However, no matter how much effort you put into trying to maintain good sleeping habits, to be successful you will occasionally be pulling all-nighters, getting up early or going to bed late so you can study, attend important meetings, or work on your personal business plan. The good news is the satisfaction you receive when you accomplish your tasks will make the reduced sleep worth it.

- Remuneration – Obtaining a higher-paying job in the short term is not necessarily the choice that will derive the financial independence you ultimately desire. In some instances it may make sense to pursue a lower-paying job, especially if it provides you with additional skills and a platform to enhance your value, which increases your long term earning power. Do not become so fixated on your short-term salary that you lose sight of attaining your long-term goals. I learned a long time ago that your self-worth ultimately determines your net-worth.

- Immediate gratification – You may have to defer instant gratification, and give up the non-essential things in your life, to focus on the tasks you need to accomplish to propel you towards your dreams. It is possible that some of your family members and friends will reach their goals sooner, and settle for where they are in life. Do not let them discourage you, because you have devised higher goals and objectives for your life. Ergo, while your outcomes may take a little longer to obtain, the rewards will be infinitely better.

- Stability – You may have to take prudent risks and temporarily live below your financial means to achieve your ultimate destiny. Albeit, in doing so you should endeavor to never put your family members or loved ones in peril. While it is okay to dream about and strive for material goods and services, such as luxury cars, big houses, and exotic vacations, remember not to become so distracted with short-term personal wants that you lose sight of your long-term objectives. Reaching your desired level of success and happiness will bring with it immense rewards and accolades.

- Relationships – It can be difficult to balance personal relationships when your heart and mind may be somewhere else. There may be times when you have to travel extensively, or relocate to a different city, state, or country, to fulfill your destiny. Establishing a serious relationship is a full-time commitment, so you have to either be all in, or out. To keep things in perspective, find a great partner that understands what you are attempting to accomplish, and is fully aligned with your endeavors. If you have that kind of support give that person the devotion and attention they deserve, without abandoning your goals and objectives.

As you embark on your journey to success, and strive to bring to fruition what you yearn for in your life, there will unquestionably be times when you have to make sacrifices.

However, do not think of a sacrifice as you having to lose something. Instead, deem a sacrifice as foregoing something of lower importance, in order to gain something of greater importance.

The good news is, while sacrifices are never pleasurable or easy, when you achieve your goals you will be extremely satisfied that you never gave up, and made the appropriate choices that contributed to your success.

"Forget about the likes and dislikes and do what must be done. For now, this is not about happiness. This is about greatness." (George Bernard Shaw, playwright, critic, political activist)

As you endure hard work, ponder tough decisions, and make difficult sacrifices, keep the faith: God will never put more on you than you can bear.

Trust that all of your efforts are preparing you for a future that is more stupendous than you ever imagined.

Life is not easy or without its troubles, and "Sometimes You Have to Lose to Win." But the encouraging news is, the harder the battles the less competition you will have, because, "If It Were Easy Everybody Would Do It."

Your present situation is not your final destination, and the best is yet to come, so keep pushing forward, because "Life Is a Journey."

# CHAPTER SEVEN

# Life Is a Journey

Your Current Situation Is Not Your Final Destination. The Best Is Yet to Come…

One day a little boy was playing outdoors and found a fascinating caterpillar. He carefully picked the caterpillar up and carried it home to show his mother. He asked his mother if he could keep the caterpillar, and she said that it would be okay as long as he took good care of it.

The little boy got a large jar from his mother and put plants to eat, and a stick to climb on, inside the jar. Every day he meticulously watched the caterpillar.

One day the caterpillar climbed up the stick and started acting strangely. The boy worriedly called his mother, who came and promptly realized that the caterpillar was creating a cocoon.

The mother explained to the boy how the caterpillar was going to go through a metamorphosis and become a butterfly.

The little boy was thrilled to hear about the changes his caterpillar would go through.

The boy watched every day, waiting for the butterfly to emerge. One day it happened: a small hole appeared in the cocoon and the butterfly started to struggle to come out.

At first, the boy was excited, but soon he became concerned. The butterfly was struggling so hard to get out. It looked like it could not break free. It appeared desperate. It seemed like the butterfly was making no progress.

The boy was so worried that he decided to help. He ran to get scissors, and snipped the cocoon to make the hole bigger. The butterfly quickly emerged.

As the butterfly came out of the cocoon the boy was surprised, because the butterfly had a swollen body and small, shriveled wings.

The boy continued to watch the butterfly, expecting that at any moment the wings would dry out, enlarge, and expand to support the swollen body.

As the days went by the boy remained hopeful that in due time the body would shrink, and the butterfly's wings would develop. But neither happened.

Unfortunately, the butterfly spent the rest of its life crawling around with a swollen body and shriveled wings. It was never able to fly.

As the boy tried to figure out what had gone wrong, his mother took him to talk to a scientist from a local college. The boy learned that as part of its journey to transform from a caterpillar, the butterfly was supposed to struggle.

In fact, the butterfly's struggle to push its way through the tiny opening of the cocoon pushes the fluid out of its body and into its wings. Without the struggle, the butterfly would never, ever fly.

Regrettably, the boy's good intentions hurt the butterfly.

Similar to a caterpillar's metamorphosis into a butterfly, this story (author unknown) is a reminder that there are comparable transformations in your life, which you must endure to reach your ultimate destiny.

A multitude of people reading this book often take the easy way out or cease making an effort, because you do not acknowledge the adversity, and impediments that you must conquer to achieve your goals and objectives.

Analogous to the butterfly that needs to struggle to escape the cocoon as it prepares itself to fly, the way in which you react to the adversity you encounter in your life will play a prominent role in determining how triumphant you will be.

Success does not happen randomly, and the challenging obstacles you confront are designed to give you the strength and confidence that is necessary to achieve your goals and objectives.

As you embark on your journey it is also crucial for you to understand that everyone's purpose in life is different.

While individuals can advise and counsel you on how they became successful, to reach your personal destiny you have to be cognizant that your life experiences will be different, because they are specifically designed for, and are unique to, you.

Other people's difficulties and misfortunes will not be the same as your complications and dilemmas. Therefore, you cannot compare your situation to someone else's.

And, although you may observe experiences that are advantegous and beneficial for another person, their encounters are not necessarily the path laid out for your life.

Just as important, you cannot expect other people to comprehend, or fully appreciate, the journey you must travel to reach the point you are destined to be at in your life.

Let me share an anecdote that will accentuate the sentiment I am expressing.

My oldest son recently graduated from Columbia Law School. While it was a momentous occasion, my son was mystified by the fact that some of his friends, who had not pursued post-graduate degrees, were predominantly focused on the six-figure starting salary he was posed to earn at a prominent New York City law firm.

However, what some of my son's friends failed to comprehend was the grueling journey he had traveled to reach this salient achievement.

On more than one occasion my son said to me: "They see the glory, but most of them do not know my story."

My son was a good high school basketball player, and selected the undergraduate college he attended primarily because he was recruited there to play basketball.

Like many young men who were talented high school basketball players, my son conjectured that his future would culminate with him being drafted into the National Basketball Association (NBA), or at a minimum playing basketball overseas, after he graduated from college.

Unfortunately, my son broke his wrist while playing in a basketball game during his sophomore year in college, and he could not play the remainder of the season.

As my son was healing from his broken wrist, and taking time away from the basketball court, it began to resonate with him that in retrospect playing professional basketball would not manifest itself in the way that he had once envisioned.

Hence, my son came to the astute conclusion that he needed to plan for an alternative scenario.

Subsequently, my son was home from college for spring break, and we were hosting a cookout for our youngest child's track team. The event included parents of the track-team members, and during the occasion my son initiated a casual conversation with one of the dads, who happened to be an attorney.

When the attorney inquired what my son was planning to do after college, my son mentioned that he was an English major, but undecided about his future. My son then inquisitively questioned the attorney about the legal profession, and what would be required to be considered for admission to a top-tier law school.

The attorney proceeded to enumerate a checklist of activities that my son needed to pursue to best position himself for admission to law school. Included on the list was pursuing a double major in English and pre-law, enhancing his GPA, and considering my son's only work experience was as a counselor for a Boys and Girls Club, the attorney suggested that my son obtain some practical business experience.

I have to admit my son took the advice to heart, adjusted his curriculum so he could double major, got serious about his academic achievements, and volunteered that summer at the Keep America Beautiful headquarters to acquire some basic business skills.

The following summer my son applied for, and earned, an internship at the U.S. Attorney's Office, where he received real-life exposure to some of the skills and qualities that are necessary to be a great lawyer.

Following graduation from college my son worked as a paralegal for a large New York law firm, where he spent a year honing his skills, before deciding to take the Law School Admission Test (LSAT) and apply to law school.

After being accepted at Columbia Law School my son spent three years as a dedicated law student, and was immersed in his studies. He curtailed his social life, and garnered internships during the summers at a couple of different law firms, to prepare himself for life after law school.

I recap my son's journey to delineate the dramatic changes and experiences he endured to manifest his dream of becoming a lawyer.

And, the story did not end there, as my son had to pass the New York State bar examination before becoming licensed to practice law as an attorney.

"Life Is a Journey," and each and every one of you will be faced with your own personal trials, tribulations, and emotional highs and lows as you travel the road to your destiny.

Yet, I encourage you to not despair. Every predicament and turn of events you encounter is preparing you for a scintillating future.

In the case of my son, breaking his wrist prompted him to contemplate his career options, which resulted in an impromptu conversation with an attorney, who encouraged my son to enhance his academic endeavors and obtain practical business experience.

The business experience and academic achievements culminated in my son receiving an internship at the U.S. Attorney's Office. The skills my son obtained working at the U.S. Attorney's Office were instrumental in him getting a paralegal position at a law firm.

My son's stint as a paralegal further engendered his interest in the legal profession, which motivated him to do well on the LSAT, resulting in my son gaining admission to Columbia Law School.

Ultimately, the scholastic achievements that my son attained at Columbia Law School, coupled with his passion and drive to excel, contributed to him being hired as an associate at one of the top law firms in America.

Far too often you fail to contemplate the challenging journey you must endure, and the transformation you have to undergo to achieve your dreams.

The journey my son traveled, and the benefits that he procured, were years in the making. Albeit, virtually everything my son encountered along the way was instrumental in shaping and molding him into the dynamic person he needed to be to fulfill his goals.

In fact, while it was not necessarily the best day of his young life, my son readily acknowledges that if he had not broken his wrist, thereby setting a number of life-changing events into motion, there is no telling how his future would have evolved.

There will undoubtedly be times in your life when you feel compelled to rationalize the reasons why some people appear to be successful in their lifelong journey, and you surmise that you are less accomplished.

I would propose a couple of provocations for you to consider.

First, as I alluded to earlier in this chapter, everyone's journey is distinct, and diverse in nature, form, and quality.

Second, some of you have circumvented your development process, and established inferior and destructive habits that are preventing you from being successful.

Many of your bad habits are not intentional, and may have even been inherited from the different environments that you were exposed to as you were growing up, but nonetheless they exist.

Let me impart a few of the debilitating habits that might be preventing you from being successful as you pursue your journey in life.

***Debilitating habits that can prevent you from being successful:***

- You lack passion, and when you encounter complications, rather than continuing to push forward, you discontinue trying, seek the easy path, and make excuses to justify your actions.

- You fail to take personal responsibility, attempt to shift blame onto factors that are supposedly outside of your control, and inculpate other people for your predicament.

- You seek instant gratification, as opposed to investing the prerequisite time and effort now, for results that will not manifest themselves until months or years later.

- You play it safe and avoid taking prudent risks, because you are afraid of failure, or do not believe your goals are attainable.

- You do not assume ownership for making things happen in your life, and fail to take advantage of appropriate opportunities.

- You lack specific goals, and are easily distracted with activities that are not beneficial to your long-term success.

- You do not learn from your previous mistakes. In some instances you continue doing the same thing over and over again, expecting a different result.

- You do not network or build beneficial relationships, and reject assistance from people who could be a positive influence and help you accomplish your aim or purpose.

Do any of the aforementioned assertions seem familiar?

The good news is that if you alter your mindset, and eradicate your deleterious behavior, all of your undesirable habits can be rectified.

"Life Is a Journey," so all of your past mistakes, and benign excuses, do not dictate your future. You can, and will, be successful if you eagerly embrace the transformation you need to go through as you move forward and pursue your destiny.

The distinguished American educator, author, orator, and advisor to presidents of the United States Booker T. Washington said, "Success is to be measured not so much by the position that one has reached in life, as by the obstacles which he has overcome while trying to succeed."

A significant number of you are in the midst of a precarious situation that seems debilitating and onerous. You do not foresee a way out of your conundrum, and are querying, "Why is it that iniquitous situations always seem to impede my progress?"

Let me convey a couple of thoughts. First, you are not alone. Each and every day people from all walks of life encounter circumstances that challenge their faith, confidence, and courage.

Do not give in to the "why me" mentality. Instead, concentrate on what you need to do to persevere, and have conviction that in the end you will prevail.

Second, you have to discern that all of your adversity is preparing you for your destiny. Through your difficulties and problems, you are overcoming your weaknesses, and becoming stronger and wiser.

It is also important for you to understand that the people who renounce you, and exit your life, are making room for the people you truly need in your life.

Yes, there will undoubtedly be times when you feel tired and despondent, and wonder if you can continue your journey and emerge victorious. Be steadfast and believe that you can conquer all of the obstacles placed in your path.

Your ultimate victory is preordained, because God gives his toughest battles to his strongest warriors.

Outlined below are a few tips you can employ to enhance your chances for success as you embark on your lifelong journey.

***Tips to enhance your chances for success:***

- Have a passion, goal, or dream that inspires and motivates you. Every day there are people achieving their objectives, and enriching their life. You need to possess the mentality that you are capable of living a blessed life, and ascending to new heights.

- Be committed to taking the necessary actions that will propel you towards your goals. Use your time wisely to garner benefits that will improve your life. There is no such thing as being too busy. If you want something bad enough you will make time for it.

- Be open to learning new skills, and acquiring inspirational insights that will enhance your current situation. Do not look back with regret, look forward with optimism. Your approach to every situation should be, "I am not where I am ultimately going to be, but I am closer today than I was yesterday."

- Develop a network of people who can contribute to your success. There is no self-made person. Everybody at one point or another has benefited from someone, or something that others did for him or her. On the other hand, remove the toxic people from your life who interfere with your dreams and/or are sabotaging your success. People can knock you down, but do not allow other people's impression of what you are, or are not, capable of achieving keep you down.

- Maintain balance in your life. Focusing all of your time and energy in any one area creates imbalance. Hence, as you pursue your goals you also need to have an outlet and participate in other activities that you enjoy.

- Learn from your successes as well as your failures. There is some merit to the concept that if you are going to fail, you should fail fast. My philosophy, however, is that learning fast will lead to success quicker than failing fast. The question you should be asking is not how fast did I fail; rather, what did I learn in the process, and what am I going to do differently as a result? Also, it is a proven fact that people who focus on both their successes and failures learn faster than people who just focus on their failures.

As I noted in the subtitle to this chapter, "Your Current Situation Is Not Your Final Destination. The Best Is Yet to Come."

Enjoy every step of the journey to your destiny, live life with a purpose, and make sure that each and every day counts.

Following is a poem entitled "You Still Have Hope," by an unknown author, which captures the essence of the messages dispensed in this chapter.

If you can look at the sunset and smile, then you still have hope.

If you can find beauty in the colors of a small flower, then you still have hope.

If you can find pleasure in the movement of a butterfly, then you still have hope.

If the smile of a child can still warm your heart, then you still have hope.

If you can see the good in other people, then you still have hope.

If the rain breaking on a rooftop can still lull you to sleep, then you still have hope.

If the sight of a rainbow still makes you stop and stare in wonder, then you still have hope.

If the soft fur of a favored pet still feels pleasant under your fingertips, then you still have hope.

If you meet new people with a trace of excitement and optimism, then you still have hope.

If you give people the benefit of the doubt, then you still have hope.

If you still offer your hand in friendship to others that have touched your life, then you still have hope.

If receiving an unexpected card or letter still brings a pleasant surprise, then you still have hope.

If the suffering of others still fills you with pain and frustration, then you still have hope.

If you refuse to let a friendship die, or accept that it must end, then you still have hope.

If you look forward to a time or place of quiet and reflection, then you still have hope.

If you still buy the ornaments, put up the Christmas tree, or cook the supper, then you still have hope.

If you can look to the past and smile, then you still have hope.

If, when faced with the bad, when told everything is futile, you can still look up and end the conversation with the phrase "yeah BUT," then you still have hope.

Hope is such a marvelous thing. It bends, it twists, it sometimes hides, but rarely does it break. It sustains us when nothing else can. It gives us reason to continue and courage to move ahead, when we tell ourselves we would rather give in.

Hope puts a smile on our face when the heart cannot manage.

Hope puts our feet on the path when our eyes cannot see it.

Hope moves us to act when our souls are confused of the direction.

Hope is a wonderful thing, something to be cherished and nurtured, and something that will refresh us in return.

And it can be found in each of us, and it can bring light into the darkest of places.

Never lose hope!


The essence of this poem is, as you journey through life, learn from your past, live in the present, and plan for your future. Everything you have experienced to date, and have yet to encounter, is preparing you for your destiny.

Above all else, do not become discouraged when your face challenges. Similar to the caterpillar that enters the cocoon and struggles to emerge as a butterfly, the struggles you encounter highlight the metamorphosis you must undergo to reach your full potential.

Be tenacious in the pursuit of your goals and dreams, and when you experience difficulties, and everything seems to be going against you, remember, "Sometimes You Have to Lose to Win."

"Life Is a Journey," so as you endure the transformation required to reach your destiny, remember to keep God first and "Manage Your Personal Brand."

CHAPTER

# Manage Your Personal Brand

Do Not Take Shortcuts, Even When No One Is Watching...

Throughout the course of my thirty-year career in corporate America, I was employed by a multitude of world-class-branded consumer packaged goods (CPG) companies. The distinguished group of companies included iconic names such as Pillsbury, Häagen-Dazs, RJR Nabisco, and PepsiCo.

One of the distinct characteristics that all of these CPG companies had in common was that each of them relied copiously on consumer branding to promote their image and merchandise their products.

Inherent in the aforementioned companies' business model was the irrefutable belief that branding went beyond merely having a recognizable logo. Consumer branding differentiated these CPG companies from their competitors, created product recognition, and facilitated a reliable reputation with their customers.

While branding is typically associated with CPG companies, I would assert that a similar concept also pertains to individuals.

Presenting yourself—or your "personal brand" as I like to refer to it—in a positive manner generates a memorable and distinct image that can be extremely advantageous to your long-term success.

Stop for a minute and think about your personal brand. All of us have one, whether you realize it or not. What do your family members, friends, colleagues, business associates, or bosses think, or say, about you when they see you, or when your name is mentioned?

Your personal brand is fundamentally what you are known for, and the differentiated traits people seek you out for.

Whether it be positive or negative how other people perceive you is a clear indication of your personal brand. Moreover, if you are not branding yourself, others will indiscriminately do it for you.

The encouraging news is, similar to CPG companies, you can refine, or change your personal brand to better reflect the person you want people to acknowledge you as.

One of the first actions you can undertake to persuade people to perceive you as the person you really are, or desire to be, is to conduct an honest assessment of your current personal brand profile. Equipped with that crucial knowledge, you can implement a plan to enhance your persona.

Let me recount a story about how one multinational company took extraordinary steps to redefine its brand image. I believe there are a few valuable insights to be gleamed from this experience that can assist you in bolstering your own personal brand.

In 2009, a YouTube video posted to the Internet showed two Domino's Pizza employees mishandling a customer's pizza, and the video went viral.

The unsavory deeds depicted in the video clearly did not reflect the virtuous image that Domino's Pizza wanted to be known for.

Subsequently, Domino's launched a massive social-media campaign to analyze the public's opinion of the Domino's brand. Not surprisingly, the campaign highlighted a number of areas where consumers felt Domino's could improve its products and service.

After assessing the undesirable feedback, Domino's made company-wide changes, including altering their pizza recipe, launching a marketing campaign acknowledging past mistakes, and promising consumers a much better product.

As a result of the business changes, coupled with the marketing campaign, Domino's Pizza saw a fourteen percent increase in sales for the quarter immediately following the rebranding crusade.

Correspondingly, Domino's stock price took off, and prompted by consumer research Domino's Pizza altered their logo, and dropped the word "pizza" from its name, to further convey it is more than a pizza chain.

By assuming control of their brand message, Domino's managed the impression they wanted stakeholders to attribute to them, which dramatically increases the odds of Domino's being recognized, and rewarded, for their endeavors.

Undoubtedly, there are people reading this book who, not dissimilar to the self-reflection Domino's went through, need to revamp their personal brand.

Perhaps you are doing everything according to your definitive plan, but people still have a misperception of who you really are, or what you stand for.

In that case, I would submit to you that one person's perception is another person's reality.

While it may not always be justified, people build an impression of you over time, and you may have to overcome incorrect perceptions to attain your goals.

As you consider the obstacles that may be hindering your path to success, what potential changes do you need to make to your personal brand?

Said another way, what specific attribute(s) do you want people to associate with you when they see you, or hear your name mentioned?

Is there a particular intellectual prowess you want to be deemed as being an expert in, or are there unassailable personal qualities you want associated with your personal brand?

As you pursue your goals and objectives, and contemplate the maturation of your personal brand, ask yourself these three questions:

- What should you continue doing?

- What should you stop doing?

- What should you start doing?

Once you ascertain, how you want to be perceived, you can begin to be much more strategic regarding how best to manage your personal brand.

Just to be abundantly clear, the personal branding I am alluding to relates to how effectively you package yourself in a way that authentically showcases your skills and talents.

Consequently, you need to always ensure the image you project is genuine and honest, because being disingenuous, unethical, or immoral will create a personal brand that will be detrimental to your long-term success and happiness.

To help you get started, here are a few idiosyncrasies I recommend you implement as you endeavor to re-brand yourself.

*Idiosyncrasies you should implement to re-brand yourself:*

- Always deliver on your promises. Create trust through consistency in your words and actions. Conduct yourself in a professional manner so people envision you in the capacity that you desire, not the position you are currently in.

- Be unique. Refine your current skill-set, and showcase all of the talents you possess. Blending in and remaining in the background will not get you noticed. Highlight the positive attribute(s) that make you distinct, and diverse. Do not overlook volunteer experiences, and other activities you participated in, which are relevant in defining your personal brand.

- Become a person who has a comprehensive, or authoritative, knowledge on an important topic, or in a specific area. Learn a new skill that expands your expertise or education. Remain current on your area of competence by participating in industry-related events, conferences, panels, or workshops to demonstrate and draw attention to your skills.

- Expand your network to encompass more people or interests. Seek out new experiences where there is ample opportunity for you to grow and develop your skills. In doing so, be clear and concise in the image you want to project. Take the time to demonstrate your passion and character. Make certain that people understand the value you possess, and why your skills are relevant.

- Leverage social media to publicize that your goals are different, and have changed immensely. Update your profile picture, refine your resume, and highlight that you are open to new opportunities and experiences.

- Monitor your image, and discern the opinions or beliefs that people have pertaining to your skills or characteristics. You need to constantly manage and fine-tune your personal brand. Therefore, ask questions along the way and take note of tendencies, or practices, that you may need to revise.

Developing a strong personal brand requires dedication and patience, and it can necessitate you undergoing a dramatic transformation to attain the results you desire.

It is also important to note that you cannot alter your image overnight. It takes time to re-brand yourself and get people to acknowledge that you have changed, and are not the person you once were.

And, even when you attain the personal brand you are seeking, you must realize that maintaining the image you desire is an evolving, never-ending process.

One negative indiscretion, or faux pas can eradicate all of your positive efforts. So be cognizant of your actions, and remember you always have to be diligent to preserve your desired personal brand image.

Another significant factor that you need to be conscious of as you shape your personal brand is the influence of social-media. The advent of the Internet has placed an appreciable priority on effectively managing your personal brand.

Each and every day, knowingly and unknowingly, you are marketing yourselves on social-media sites. Albeit, the representation may not be exactly what you would expect, or desire it to be.

Google yourself, or go on Facebook, Twitter, or LinkedIn, and you might be surprised by what is revealed when your name is divulged.

While some people are very adept at utilizing social media to portray themselves in a distinguished manner, other individuals are destroying their image, and creating a personal brand that could be extremely detrimental to their long-term success.

In today's society, it is not uncommon for future employers, colleagues, or potential business associates to access social-media platforms to ascertain the persona that your personal brand projects.

Hence, you have to proactively stay current on the impression your personal brand is projecting on social-media.

Allow me to share with you a few examples of social-media impressions that can be detrimental to your personal, and professional, relationships.

*Social-media impressions that can be detrimental:*

- While you may not always be able to control someone posting an unflattering photo of you on social-media, you personally sharing a picture of yourself doing a keg stand, or making an obscene gesture to the camera, etc., could have a deleterious effect on your personal brand.

- Making discriminating comments, bullying, or posting cartoons and quotes that are hateful toward someone else's race, religious beliefs, or sexual orientation is an unequivocal way to decimate your personal brand.

- Sharing company secrets, or discussing workplace issues that portray your employer, fellow colleagues, or business associates in an uncomplimentary light, raises serious doubt about you having discernment or good judgment.

- Posting pictures of yourself at a baseball game when you called into work hacking and coughing, while pretending to be sick, undermines your credibility.

- Complaining about past employers on social media is a definite red flag to any potential employer, or business associate, that you could be trouble down the road. If you are quick to humiliate other people, why should they trust that you would not do the same to them at some point?

- Posting a resume on a social-media account that does not accurately represent your accomplishments. Or, having critical information posted on the Web, such as a criminal record, which you did not reveal in an interview or business agreement, could imply that you are less than truthful in all of your endeavors.

I would also venture to say that while having an egregious social-media profile can be damaging, not having a social-media profile presence can also be an issue, as it may suggest you are hiding something, or are not tech savvy.

We have reached a point in our society where social-media, and your personal brand, are so interwoven into your life that you can oftentimes forget that every single thing you do is not suitable to be shared.

To be judicious you have to assume that everything posted on social-media is accessible to the masses, and can tarnish your personal brand, thereby derailing you from reaching your destiny.

Along with being conscience of your personal brand, another pitfall you must be mindful of is not being able to flex your style, or adjust to new conditions and circumstances.

Being unable, or unwilling, to change, typically in a comparatively small but significant way, can result in your losing a beneficial opportunity that may be instrumental in helping you achieve your goals.

Some of you reading this book probably know of a person who struggles to accept, learn, or use new processes and technology.

As a result, they are confined in their current situation due to their reluctance to flex their style, acclimate to the latest trends, and acquire new skills.

I would postulate that the old saying: " You can't teach an old dog new tricks" is completely false. Especially when that premise is applied to human beings.

To be successful at anything you are pursuing in life, one of the most important skills you have to develop is the ability to be flexible, and adapt to change.

You can never stop learning and must be inquisitive about new and different concepts. Otherwise, you will be relegated to a dismal life that does not culminate in you fulfilling your destiny.

To quote English naturalist and geologist Charles Darwin, "It is not the strongest species that survive, nor the most intelligent, but the ones most responsive to change."

Following is a short story entitled "Grow Great by Dreams" (by author unknown), which augments the point Charles Darwin was making in his quote.

The question was once asked of a highly successful businessman, "How have you done so much in your lifetime?"

The businessman replied, "I have dreamed. I have turned my mind loose to imagine what I wanted to do. Then I have gone to bed and thought about my dreams. And, when I awoke in the morning I saw the way to make my dreams real. While other people were saying, 'You can't do that, it isn't possible,' I was well on my way to achieving what I wanted."

To quote Woodrow Wilson, 28th president of the United States, "We grow great by dreams. All big men are dreamers. They see things in the soft haze of a spring day, or in a red fire on a long winter's evening."

The businessman went on to say, "Some of us let great dreams die, but others nourish and protect them; nourish them through bad days until they bring them to the sunshine and light, which always comes to those who sincerely hope that their dreams will come true. So please, do not let anyone steal your dreams, or try to tell you they are too impossible. Sing your song, dream your dreams, hope your hope, and pray your prayer."

How many of you, in lieu of making a subtle yet impactful change that could invigorate your personal brand and magnify your life, allow someone to steal your dreams, or tell you your dreams are impossible.

Constantly reinvigorating your life, and implementing the modifications required to accommodate your goals and objectives, is imperative to your long-term success and happiness.

Allow me to share another small example of how making diminutive adjustments, and managing your personal brand, can be advantageous.

When my family goes out to dinner at a fine dining restaurant, I typically wear a sport coat or blazer, and if my sons are with me, they dress that way as well.

Surprisingly (or maybe not so surprisingly), the level of service that we typically receive is different when we wear jackets compared to when we do not.

While some might suggest the enhanced service is a figment of my imagination, I will confess the supplementary service that we experience may be a minor variation, but nonetheless it is something I have become astutely aware of.

Furthermore, I would hypothesize a rationale for the contrasting service that we experience is partly due to the personal brand image we exhibit.

Think about it. You feel emboldened when you are dressed up, and that confident, positive feeling is subsequently projected to the people you encounter.

Likewise, people employed in restaurants are predisposed, through their prior experiences, to believe people who are wearing business attire, or out for a special occasion, provide better remuneration.

Hence, the level or quality of service you receive is often analogous to your personal brand image.

My purpose here is not to postulate that merely wearing a specific type of clothing is the key to receiving extraordinary service in a restaurant. The premise is, your actions very often dictate, and impact, how other people react toward you.

How you walk, how you talk, what you wear is all part of your personal brand, and influence how others perceive you.

Allow me to be crystal clear about the observation I just made. I am not for a moment suggesting that you are obligated to change who you are, and what you stand for, to accommodate other people.

However, you do need to understand that flexing your style, and leveraging your personal brand, when it is appropriate, can be instrumental in helping you achieve your desired results.

Flexing your style does not have to result in you making wholesale changes. Flexing your style can be as simple as starting with the behavior you are most comfortable with, and then adjusting your persona to gradually adapt, when it is suitable or proper in the circumstances, to what is required for you to accomplish your objective(s).

You do not need to totally relinquish your values to accommodate another person, just improvise and modify your behavior, when it makes sense, to achieve your coveted outcome.

More often than not, nothing dramatic is required to tweak your approach to various situations. Remember, you are always in control of how you respond to any predicament, and can choose your behavior.

It is always okay to say *"no"* to an endeavor, or way of thinking, which is not consistent with your values. Nevertheless, do not use something you do not want to do as an excuse for not doing something that needs to be done.

Learning to flex your style takes practice and awareness, but if the outcome you want to achieve is important to you, it is well worth the effort.

Earlier in the book I wrote about emulating success. While adapting the traits of successful people can be advantageous you also have to be conscious of your personal brand, and retain your own unique style in the process.

Yes, you should have mentors and role models. And, you should observe them and learn from them. Just ensure you do not blindly follow them. You need to always maintain your own individual personality, values, and beliefs.

A few years ago, I received an e-mail from a woman who described her fiancé as a guy who, in her words, "Spends a lot of time watching self-help videos and listening to motivational speakers, and I feel like he relies on everyone else to give him answers on the key to his personal success."

She went on to say, "I know his heart is in the right place, but fear holds him back. I can't put my finger on exactly what that is, but he is definitely scared of something. I just don't know how I can support him in a way that gives him the courage to accomplish what he says he wants."

She concluded her e-mail by asking, "Can you please offer any advice that can help me figure my fiancé out, so I can support him in being all that he is capable of?

I am not a psychologist, and there may be a number of complex issues contributing to this particular situation, but after giving it some thought, the gist of my response to the woman was threefold.

First, I conveyed that her fiancé has to come to grips with the reality that other people can inspire and motivate him, but ultimately he has to personally put forth the intense desire, determination, and dedication required to accomplish his dreams and aspirations.

The reality is that people who are underachievers tend to seek out people who tell them what they want to hear, rather than listening to people who tell them what they need to hear.

This woman's fiancé watching self-help videos, and listening to motivational speakers, was a way to make it appear as if he was interested in being successful, yet at the same time he avoided making a commitment, or accepting personal responsibility, because he did not have anyone holding him accountable to implement the changes he needed to make.

Second, her fiancé is afraid of failing and needs to understand that fear is a natural occurrence. The key is not to let fear consume you, and prevent you from doing things that will contribute to your success and happiness.

When you decide to face your fears, you can willingly and enthusiastically pursue your goals and objectives.

Third, while there are lessons that you can learn from other people, there is indubitably no secret formula to success. Everyone's path to success is unique and personal, and involves hard work, sacrifice, and extraordinary effort.

In this case, it appears her fiancé was more infatuated by other people's personal brand, and their story of success, than he was in developing his own personal brand and success story.

I concluded my response to the woman by telling her that as much as she loved her fiancé, she cannot do for him what he does not want to do, or is unwilling to do, for himself.

The takeaways from this exchange are you should be inspired by the success of others and attempt to learn from their experiences and insights, but at the same time you must realize that your personal brand, and path to success, will be as distinctive as each star in the sky.

Everyone's personal brand and journey in life is different, and it is impossible to exactly emulate someone else's success to achieve your own personal success.

In the words of the famous American singer, actress, and vaudevillian Judy Garland, "Always be a first-rate version of yourself, instead of a second-rate version of somebody else."

MANAGE YOUR PERSONAL BRAND

As you commence the journey toward your destiny remember to always "Manage Your Personal Brand," and do not spend your precious time fixated on "Would Have, Could Have, Should Have."

151

# CHAPTER NINE

# Would Have, Could Have, Should Have

Do Not Allow Your Past to Decimate the Present, or Dominate Your Future…

It always amazes me when I hear people say, "If I had to do it all over again I would not change a thing." Is that really true?

According to the legendary sports figure, philanthropist, and social activist Muhammad Ali, "The man who views the world at fifty the same as he did at twenty has wasted thirty years of his life."

I have thoroughly enjoyed my life, but readily admit I have made a number of gaffes over the years.

Hence, if it were possible to do things all over again, I hope I would be perspicacious enough not to make the same mistakes, albeit I would probably create some new ones.

# WOULD HAVE, COULD HAVE, SHOULD HAVE

The title of this chapter, "Would Have, Could Have, Should Have," is a metaphor for all of the things that you wish you had done differently in your life.

Although it can be soothing to envision going back in time and changing the past, the truth is you have to acknowledge the state of situations as they actually exist, as opposed to having an idealistic or notional idea of them.

If you become overly fixated on the quixotic notion of "Would Have, Could Have, Should Have," it will result in you living a life filled with regrets, and you will not fulfill your destiny.

In the 1985 science-fiction comedy film *Back to the Future*, directed by Robert Zemeckis and written by Zemeckis and Bob Gale, a small-town California teenager, Marty McFly, is thrown back in time when an experiment by his eccentric scientist friend, Doc Brown, goes amiss.

The film stars Michael J. Fox as teenager Marty McFly, and Christopher Lloyd portrays the eccentric scientist Dr. Emmett "Doc" Brown. The premise of the story is that Doc developed a time machine (a modified DeLorean car), which allows Marty to travel through time where he encounters young versions of his parents, and must make sure that they fall in love, or Marty will cease to exist.

For the few of you who have not seen the movie, I will not divulge the ending; however, I will say this movie became a worldwide cultural phenomenon, and fostered a trilogy of "Back to the Future" films.

While a fair number of people reading this book would probably like to hit the rewind button and go back in time like Marty McFly, that is an unrealistic and impractical proposition, because the reality is that rarely, if ever, do you get a do-over.

In fact, one of the few instances where you might receive a do-over, or mulligan, is in the game of golf. In some informal golf games, a player is ceremoniously given a second chance to replay his or her golf shot, usually after the first chance went awry.

And, it is noteworthy that although a mulligan occasionally occurs in a casual golf game played between friends, a mulligan is not actually permitted in the formal rules of golf.

In real life, in lieu of going "Back to the Future" or receiving a mulligan, you have to start from where you are, and make a new beginning, with an enhanced and advantageous ending.

Too often you utilize your intellectual capacity denying the reality of your current situation, rather than assessing your circumstances, and developing the appropriate response.

There comes a point in your life when you have to stop thinking about what is gone, appreciate what still remains, and look forward to what is yet to come.

Encapsulating yourself in a world where you constantly reiterate, what you "Would Have, Could Have, Should Have" did will not propel you to the awesome future that is awaiting you.

# WOULD HAVE, COULD HAVE, SHOULD HAVE

Yes, you should definitely learn from your prior experiences, but hindsight is twenty-twenty, and invariably leads to you mulling over things you wish you had not done, or things you did not do, but wish you had.

How many times have you found yourself reflecting back over your past, saying or thinking something akin to...?

- I wish I had gone to college, or finished college.

- I wish I had chosen another career.

- I wish I had saved more money.

- I wish I had been a better parent.

- I wish I had taken better care of my health.

- I wish I had stayed in touch with my friends.

- I wish I had helped a stranger in need, or gotten involved with a local charity.

- I wish I had traveled more.

- I wish I had started my own business.

- I wish I had not worried so much about all of the things I wish I had done.

- Etc., etc.

People who stare wistfully at the past invariably have their backs turned to the future. Said another way, spending time looking remorsefully back over your past pursuits prevents you from taking judicious actions that can enhance the present and aggrandize your future.

"When one door closes another door opens, but we often look so regrettably upon the closed door that we do not see the one which has opened for us." (Alexander Graham Bell, scientist, inventor, engineer, and innovator)

A simplistic way to eradicate your "I wish I had" list is to focus on what you need to do to augment your future.

Failure does not come from falling down. Failure comes from not getting up when you fall. Ergo, do not allow your previous shortcomings to overshadow today. Instead, use your past experiences to create a better tomorrow.

One of the first action steps you should undertake to help you relinquish the obsession with your past is to objectively assess your life. When were you the happiest, and comparatively what circumstances contributed to you reaching your lowest point?

Also, think carefully about the attributes that were instrumental in making you feel motivated, and excited about your future.

Finally, examine methodically, and in excruciating detail, what you learned about yourself in the good situations, as well as the unpleasant circumstances.

In particular, what uplifting habits do you want to replicate going forward, and what inferior behaviors do you want to eradicate, because they are no longer useful, or desirable?

I have learned that in your life you can have results, or excuses. But, you cannot have both and be successful.

"Do or do not. There is no try." (Master Yoda – Star Wars)

Therefore, it is essential that as you contemplate your future, you think about what you want to accomplish, and ask yourself what is preventing you from turning your life around. Why can't you...?

- Enroll in college, or complete the college degree you started.

- Receive a promotion or obtain a better job.

- Change your career.

- Save money and become financially secure.

- Spend more time with your loved ones.

- Exercise, eat better, and receive the necessary medical attention you require.

- Reunite with old friends and make new friends.

- Volunteer and support a cause you are passionate about.

- Secure a corporate board seat.

- Start your own business.

- Etc., etc.

I advise people to go through this salient exercise because I believe you learn just as much, if not more, from acknowledging your perceived failures as you do from celebrating your successes.

As you formulate the future you desire for yourself and your family members, you need to start by making practical and effective use of the resources you have available to you, versus complaining about what you do not have.

What you deem to be insufficient can become significant if it is utilized in the right way.

While you may not realize it, most successful people did not start out with an abundance of money, a network of mentors, or the prerequisite qualities and characteristics that ultimately contributed to their success.

A multitude of people that you would probably acknowledge as being successful commenced their journey with nothing of importance or significance, and believed that through their diligence, positive attitude, and persistence it would evolve into something greater.

How many times have you thought about your future and said to yourself, or maybe even communicated to someone else...?

- I am too old, too young, not the right gender, or do not have the compulsory ethnic background.

- I am not smart or talented enough, and am afraid of what I do not know.

- I was not born in the right neighborhood, or into the appropriate family.

- I do not have mentors or people who will support me. What will people say about me if I attempt to do this?

- I do not have enough time to figure out what I need to do.

- I do not know if I will succeed. What if it does not work out?

- I do not have the money required to do this.

- I will start tomorrow.

- Etc., etc.

Starting today, you need to possess the dauntless faith that you have enough of whatever you need to get started, and more will avail itself to you along your journey.

You are talented and competent. You are ingenious and resourceful. You are tenacious and purposeful. You are a victor and not a victim.

Stop allowing pessimistic, defeatist thinking to prevent you from initiating the changes that need to be implemented in your life.

Trust in yourself, eliminate the excuses, and believe that you have the unalienable right, and the worthiness, to live your life as you envision it. Do not allow a negative mindset or naysayers to hold you back.

Throughout this book I have shared insights on overcoming adversity, and achieving your personal goals and objectives.

At this stage, I want to touch on a subject that far too often plays a prominent role in derailing people as they pursue their destiny.

Specifically, I am referring to money management and financial responsibility.

What I am going to convey will be uncomfortable for some of the readers of this book, but I have personally observed so many people use money as an excuse for underachieving, and not fulfilling their destiny, that the misconceptions about money have to be addressed.

On more than one occasion I have heard people exclaim the expression "Money is the root of all evil." This type of mindset can become an acceptable excuse, since in essence what the person(s) were saying is, "I would be a better person if I were poor, because money causes nothing but problems."

While I do not intend to engage in a theological debate about evil or its roots, I would propose that the mantra "Money is the root of all evil" is misquoted from a biblical source. 1 Timothy 6:10 (New International Version) proclaims, "For the love of money is a root of all kinds of evil."

Notice the slight difference? The verse refers to the love of money, not money itself, as being the root of all kinds of evil, not all evil. A few small words can make a big difference.

If you are totally committed to augmenting your life, and cannot think of any way to provide value or be of service to someone else, then you are hindered by the biggest excuse of all: the excuse that money is the source, and root, of all the problems in your life.

The truth is, your assessment that money, or lack thereof, is the culprit responsible for your shortcomings is erroneous. Money is not your issue. However, what is deficient, or inadequate, is your lack of understanding of your vast capabilities, talents, and gifts, and how you can be of value to others.

Regardless of who you are and what your life experiences have been, you have something vital to offer that others deem essential, or very important, and will compensate you for.

Bill Gates, the cofounder of Microsoft and a renowned entrepreneur, philanthropist, and investor, was quoted as saying, "If you're born poor it's not your mistake. But if you die poor, it's your mistake."

If money has been the primary reason why you have not pursued your goals and objectives, I encourage you to rebuke that mentality. You need to understand that the more you empower yourself to take control of any situation, the more you will enhance your ability to add value, and thereby increase your remuneration.

Now, to be totally balanced I am not advocating that amassing money is easy; that is far from the truth. The point I am elucidating is that to be successful in any aspect of your life, you have to eliminate the hypothesis that you cannot, or will not, be successful merely because you lack money.

For far too long many of you have used money as an excuse for not doing something, not experiencing something, and not pursuing your dreams.

Worse yet, you have allowed other people to use the leverage of money to make you a victim, and prevent you from attaining what is rightfully yours.

I beseech you not to be the victim anymore. Do not allow the fear associated with not having money, or the insecurity of your current financial situation, to curtail you from fulfilling your destiny.

Due to its complexity, the money protestation is not something that I can easily rectify in one chapter of a book. Nonetheless, to help you get started in improving your financial situation, I will provide a few fundamental tips.

*Tips to improve your financial situation:*

- Stop dwelling on the previous mistakes you made managing money. Yes, you should definitely learn from your past money management errors and misjudgments, but make a commitment to turning over a new leaf, and be positive about how you are going to preside over your money going forward.

- Institute a budget to help you gain a better grasp of how much money you are spending for your various endeavors. Set goals so you know exactly the amount of money you have available to spend, and how it will be utilized.

- Understand the difference between gross pay and net pay. Gross pay is the amount that you earn. More importantly, net pay is the amount that you actually take home after taxes, benefits, and other voluntary deductions are subtracted from your wages. Budget your spending based on your net pay, not your gross pay.

- Devise a plan to help you remediate past financial woes. Paying off huge credit-card debt, or recovering from a bankruptcy, will take time and diligence. Although, it is doable if you stay on track and remain within your established budget.

- Learn to live on what you earn. Identify opportunities to reduce your expenditures by living more simply. Particularly, eliminate your impulse spending, and cut back on non-essential expenses, such as cable and Internet, subscriptions, club memberships, and vacation expenditures.

- Pay yourself first. Participate in a 401k plan if it is available where you are employed, or use automatic savings withdrawal from your paycheck to set aside money. The best time to save money is when you have money. Take baby steps if you have to, but definitely start to accumulate money for your future.

- Seek ways to enhance the amount of money you earn. Negotiate for a higher salary, take on a second job, or do side projects that will allow you to bring in more passive income.

- View earning, saving, and managing your money as a beneficial experience that you take delight or pleasure in doing. Gaining control of your finances should be a positive emotion, not something that you have anxiety about.

- Ensure you have an adequate amount of savings set aside in case of emergencies. Employ separate savings accounts for your savings, expenses, and emergency funds. Maintain financial discipline and put some money out of easy reach to avoid the impulse to spend money when you do not actually need to.

- Gain alignment with your spouse or significant other in terms of setting financial goals and deploying when, and how, money will be spent. Also, when it comes to a financial decision that involves spending large sums of money, wait, think about it, do some research, and then decide.

- Shop around for the best credit cards and interest rates. Also, seek financial guidance from a qualified and trusted advisor to assist you in meeting your money management goals.

- Learn to say *"no."* If giving assistance to family members or friends is forcing you into financial peril, politely notify them that you can help in other ways, but are not in a position to give them money. You must take care of your own financial security before assisting others.

The aforementioned tips are by no means intended to be comprehensive. This list does, however, provide an excellent place for you to start.

As you consider the steps that you need to undertake to make noticeable improvement in your future, it is important to remember that being a good financial steward is not an all or nothing proposition.

You can make progress on your financial goals without committing to complete frugality, massive saving, or working three jobs.

By focusing on just a few of the caveats outlined above, you can begin to eradicate the notion of money being the reason you are not making progress toward your stated goals and objectives.

Life is full of endless possibilities. Therefore, you cannot allow self-doubt, or a "Would Have, Could Have, Should Have" mentality, to anchor you in a place that is not conducive to where you were destined to be.

You are a victor, not a victim, so renounce the regrets you may be dealing with that occurred in your past, and grasp the opportunities that will enlighten your future.

Here is a quote I read (author unknown) which captures the crux of what was conveyed in this chapter.

"Doubt sees the obstacles. Faith sees the way. Doubt sees the darkest night. Faith sees the day. Doubt dreads to take a step. Faith soars on high. Doubt questions, who believes? Faith answers, I."

The pivotal question you have to answer is, are you going to capitulate to your past, and remain fixated on what you "Would Have, Should Have, Could Have" done? Or, are you going to embrace your future and do what needs to be done? "It Is All Up to You."

# It Is All Up to You

Every Tomorrow Has Two Handles; You Can Take Hold of It by the Handle of Anxiety, or by the Handle of Faith…

Throughout the multifarious chapters in this book, I have disseminated stories of people who have overcome adversity, eradicated obstacles, and reversed losses to accomplish their goals and attain the destiny that God has planned for their life.

However, the final and most noteworthy story has not been written yet, because that narrative relates to the incredible feats that will culminate from the journey on which you are currently embarking.

*Sometimes You Have to Lose to Win* was written to be an inspirational message, and instructional strategy, that propels you to activate your dreams and aspirations.

This book was also composed to encourage you to cease focusing on all of the things that could possibly go wrong, and start celebrating how exhilarating it will be when it all goes right.

Life is enthralled with wins and losses, joy and sadness, and successes and challenges.

Rather than becoming despondent, you need to realize that "Sometimes You Have to Lose to Win," because it is as a result of your trials and tribulations that you discover what is required for you to be victorious.

Through your lifelong journey you will become more enlightened as you acquire additional knowledge, and secure advantageous outcomes from your various encounters.

Behind you is infinite power, in front of you are endless possibilities, and around you are boundless opportunities.

Therefore, you need to learn from both your setbacks and your successes, while having the confidence that everything you aspire to effectuate in your life is feasible.

In spite of what people may say, or do, in an effort to derail you from reaching your destiny, do not become disillusioned and lose your courage or enthusiasm.

Your purpose in life is to accomplish phenomenal things, and ascend to monumental heights.

Gaiety, exuberance, financial independence, triumphs, and accolades are rightfully yours to claim, and are encompassed in your destiny.

"It Is All Up to You" to manifest in your life everything that you are worthy of, and unequivocally deserve.

I wholeheartedly believe the most predominant reason that you do not presume it is possible for you to obtain what you desire, is because throughout your life you have heard more about what you are not capable of, than you have received encouragement, relative to the success that you could attain.

The fact is, people have put invisible constraints on your dreams and ambitions, and you are fostering that conclusion by settling for less, and being complacent, versus living the awe-inspiring life that is intended for you.

Even as you read this book, some of you are having self-doubt, and fear that if you actively pursue your goals and objectives, something bad or unpleasant will happen.

You are encapsulated in your comfort zone, and do not believe you can experience the euphoria I accentuated because you have been conditioned to expect, and accept, melancholy outcomes.

Allow me to share with you a poem, written by an unknown writer, which defines the perils of not venturing out of your comfort zone.

## *My Comfort Zone*

I used to have a comfort zone

Where I knew I would not fail

The same four walls and busywork

Were really more like jail

I longed so much to do the things I had never done before

But stayed inside my comfort zone

And paced the same old floor

I said it did not matter that I was not doing much

I said I did not care for things like helping others and such

I claimed to be so busy with the things inside my zone

But deep inside I longed for something special of my own

I could not let life go by just watching others win

I held my breath; I stepped outside and let the change begin

I took a step with new strength I had never felt before

I kissed my comfort zone goodbye

And closed, and locked the door

If you are in a comfort zone, afraid to venture out

Remember that all winners were at one time filled with doubt

A step or two and words of praise

Can make your dreams come true

Reach for your future with a smile; success is there for you

This poem is a lucid reminder that everything you desire in your life is obtainable. Nothing big ever comes from thinking small, so to commence your transformation process you first and foremost have to step outside of your comfort zone.

The irony is, it is often better to attempt something and fail than to try nothing and succeed.

And, if you do not dream bigger, and expect more, then you will continue to be deprived of the things that you cherish most.

I would even go so far as to say, the principal impediments to your success and happiness are the ones that you place on yourself. Life is not happening to you, life is responding to you.

The question you have to ask yourself is, "Why should other people be happy, content, and prosperous and you are not?"

The people you admire or hold in high esteem are not smarter, more entitled, or more virtuous than you.

The fundamental difference between people who have achieved their aim or purpose in life, and those who do not, is that successful people have a higher expectation that they will be victorious, while unsuccessful people accept losing as their designated position in life.

I am articulating this message not in an attempt to chastise or admonish you. To the contrary, my sole purpose for sharing these insights is to embolden you, by emphasizing what is possible in your life.

Knowing and believing that you are truly blessed, and highly favored, is a powerful revelation that will catapult you into the awesome life that you were intended to live.

It does not matter what occurred in your past, or your current economic or personal status; you are destined for greatness.

Everything that you seek and desire in your life is possible and achievable. The key is to believe in yourself and your God-given abilities.

This may be a debatable concept for some people, but it is a proven fact that you limit what you are capable of accomplishing when you have low expectations.

Alternatively, if you have great expectations you believe something good will come your way.

Allow me to recount an event that might help you put what I am saying in perspective.

In 1954, Roger Bannister ran a mile in three minutes and 59.4 seconds. This is noteworthy, because up to that point in time running a mile under four minutes had never been accomplished.

In fact, medical experts had previously said it was impossible; the human body was not capable of running a mile under four minutes.

Less than a year after Roger Bannister's exploit, another man ran a mile in less than four minutes. Subsequently, other runners were successful in running a mile in less than four minutes as well.

Today, running a mile in less than four minutes is considered routine, as even top high school runners achieve this feat.

I truly believe the primary reason Roger Bannister was able to accomplish this achievement, which heretofore had been deemed impossible, was because he believed in his God-given abilities, and did not limit himself or his expectations.

Just as importantly, once Roger Bannister ran the mile under four minutes, other runners throughout the world started to comprehend that what they had come to believe was impossible, was indeed possible.

Most of you reading this book probably do not aspire to run a sub-four-minute mile, but that is not my point.

I relate this story because it demonstrates that if you unabatedly believe in yourself, dream big dreams, work diligently, and expect the unexpected, majestic things happen.

With desire, dedication, and determination, you have it within you to accomplish goals and objectives that other people may perceive as impossible.

Success is not a destination, it is an effective mindset, and necessitates you having the attitude that you can attain the recognition and achievements in life that personally matter most to you.

In writing this book, I want to exhort you not to settle into an existence that is markedly below what is possible for you, or worse yet be diffident and not vehemently pursue your goals and dreams.

The fact of the matter is you have one thing in common with all successful people: twenty-four hours in a day. It is how you use those twenty-four hours that makes all the difference.

Hence, it is imperative that you are passionate about your goals and aspirations; success does not happen by accident, it happens on purpose.

I believe that repetition enhances the learning process and makes an idea clearer: so allow me to briefly recap a few of the valuable life lessons that we have discussed throughout this book.

*Valuable life lessons that you can benefit from:*

- The fear that emanates when you make significant changes, or face new challenges, is a natural occurrence. It is how you channel your fear that determines whether or not you will be successful. Inevitably, there will be obstacles that impede your path, but engage them with confidence. Do not be afraid to take chances and constructively pursue your goals. Your life is infused with new and bold possibilities, and you are capable of navigating through any challenge you face. As the Charismatic Christian author and speaker Joyce Meyer says, "You cannot have a testimony without having a test." Believing that it is your destiny to overcome your consternation and make a significant difference, not just for yourself, but also for your loved ones, is critical to your succeeding in anything you attempt to accomplish.

- If you become complacent and satisfied with where you are currently at in your life, you will never progress to where you are destined to be. When you reach the top of one hill, you cannot become satisfied and settle for where you are. You have to maintain a positive mindset, and extreme fortitude, because to achieve your goals there are other hills and mountains to climb. Here is a quote, by an unknown author, that exemplifies the point I am making: "If you do not make the time to work on creating the life you want, you are eventually going to be forced to spend a lot of time with a life you do not want." As you pursue your destiny you need to maintain a positive mentality, and never give up on yourself, or your ambitious goals, until you have no more of yourself to give.

- There is a fallacy that exists which assumes everyone who is successful made it on his or her own, without any assistance, counsel, or guidance. If you follow that misguided perception, you will become reluctant to seek out the people or resources that could be instrumental in helping you achieve your destiny. I can assure you everybody that has achieved greatness received support, or advice at some point along the way. You cannot be reluctant to pursue the mentorships and endorsements that are required to boost your likelihood for a triumphant outcome. Also, be mindful of the fact that if you treat other people equitably and fairly, there is a very high probability that they will respond to you in the same manner.

- Blaming other people, or allowing someone else to determine your fate, is a definite "no-no" if you are going to be successful in any endeavor. You need to dismiss the errant belief that everything that happens to you is unfair, outside of your control, and someone else's fault. Your end result is directly proportionate to the amount of commitment, diligence, and effort you put forth. Embrace the challenges you encounter with a clear understanding that there are no shortcuts on the road to success. To be victorious and attain your goals, you invariably have to hold yourself accountable for what occurs in your life, and do whatever it takes to navigate through your problems and difficulties.

- Bemoaning your current predicament, and complaining about how your life should be different, is detrimental, and will not bestow on you the success you are seeking. The reality is, you will have a difficult time making it through today if you are still carrying the burdens from yesterday. Acknowledge your opportunity areas, but also trust and believe in yourself, and forgive yourself for what you do not know, and the mistakes you have made. Relinquish the past, embrace the future, confront your problems, and stop perceiving yourself as a hopeless victim. Above all else, keep moving forward with the faith and optimism that all of the missteps you previously encountered will serve you well in your future.

- There is an old saying, "If you do not know where you are going any road will get you there." To reach your destiny you need to have a detailed plan that outlines your priorities and desired results. Be intently focused on the goals and objectives that are most important in your life, and do not allow distractions, obstacles, or other people's perceptions to derail you from your intended destination. Having a well-thought-out plan also entails having clearly defined boundaries, and learning to say "no" to errant behaviors, and ways of thinking, which are inconsistent with your master plan. Each of us will leave a legacy behind in this lifetime; the question you have to answer is, "What will your legacy be?"

A fundamental component of your personal success is living each day with the attitude that you deserve every favorable, and advantageous, opportunity that comes your way.

Entrepreneur, author, and motivational speaker Jim Rohn had numerous famous quotes, including this one: "Let others lead small lives, but not you... Let others leave their future in someone else's hand, but not you."

The truth is, since the day that you were born an aspect of your destiny was to live a happy, abundant, prolific life.

With that thought in mind, have you ever noticed how a four-year-old child will attempt almost anything? They are unencumbered and have no fear.

Unlike adults, who look at new opportunities and focus their attention on all of the things that could possibly go wrong, young children are full of hope and innocence, and believe anything is possible.

To achieve your destiny, and accomplish feats that some people would deem to be impossible, you have to act and conduct yourself like a mature adult, but have the optimism of an energetic child.

Trust that God has a majestic plan for your life, and any appalling circumstances you encounter, or difficult situation you are going through, is only temporary.

When you are faced with a formidable challenge, have to make a crucial decision, or encounter an unorthodox predicament, expect supernatural forces to intercede on your behalf.

Believing you are highly favored, and entitled to the utmost that life has to offer, is a divine mindset, and a spiritually aware way to envision your life. And, it will transform your perspective on what happens for you, and to you.

Accordingly, in the event that you do not receive the outcome you covet, anticipate greater, and believe something exceedingly better is forthcoming.

I do not want to be overzealous and suggest that every situation you encounter will always be easy. In fact, it is quite the contrary.

Notable results do not happen overnight, and you unequivocally need to be faithful, and exhibit the prerequisite desire, determination, and dedication, to achieve positive outcomes.

Consequently, in the midst of any dire situation you face, believing that you can, and will, prevail, is the key ingredient that separates champions from people who fail to reach their full potential.

As opposed to commiserating about what you cannot do, you need to embrace all of the tremendous possibilities that are accessible to you.

The best is yet to come!

Therefore, believe in yourself and alter your negative mindset, and as a result you will embellish your life.

The following poem entitled "Believe in Yourself" (author unknown) reflects the attitude you have to exhibit to be successful in any venture.

## *Believe in Yourself*

Believe in yourself and in your dream

Though impossible things may seem

Someday, somehow you'll get through

To the goal you have in view

Mountains fall and seas divide

Before the one who in his stride

Takes a hard road day by day

Sweeping obstacles away

Believe in yourself and in your plan

Say not I cannot but I can

The prizes of life we fail to win

Because we doubt the power within

The unpretentious words in this poem can have powerful results if you activate them in your life.

I am living proof that believing in yourself, especially when other people do not believe in you, can culminate into monumental outcomes.

Let me offer one final piece of sage advice. Some people might be predisposed to conjecture that having an expectation of success and abundance is synonymous with being cocky and arrogant.

I would respectfully disagree and advocate that having confidence, and believing in your abilities, is quite the contrary to being haughty.

If you take the prerequisite steps to prepare you to realize the goals and objectives you desire to achieve, you should unequivocally be self-assured.

Constantly remind yourself that you are worthy, capable, and above all truly blessed and highly favored. Prosperity is your rightful reward and you deserve to emerge victorious.

"It Is All Up to You" to grasp the opportunities placed before you, and fulfill your destiny.

From this day forward, have confidence in your abilities, live your dreams, step out on faith, and exceed everyone's expectations, including your own.

SOMETIMES YOU HAVE TO LOSE TO WIN

I sincerely believe that if you adhere to the principals articulated throughout the various chapters in this book, you will be bold enough to use your voice, brave enough to listen to your heart, and wise enough to activate your goals and aspirations, so you can live the life that you have always imagined.

My unassailable wish for you is that all of your awe-inspiring ambitions are realized. Believe it in your mind, receive it in your soul, and achieve it in your life.

Your current situation is not your final destination. Consequently, do not allow yourself to agonize over the difficulties and misfortunes you encounter on your journey.

Take pride in the great distance you have already come, and have undeniable faith in how far you can still go, because the best is yet to come.

Above and beyond all other considerations, as you embark on your lifelong odyssey, trust in God, and envision that you can be, and will be, successful in all of your endeavors.

I trust that you have enjoyed reading this book and pray that it will serve as an indispensable guide to help you live your life in such a way that all of your dreams come true.

Be encouraged, keep the faith, and become adept in "How to Conquer Adversity and Fulfill Your Destiny," because "Sometimes You Have to Lose to Win."

# Bibliography

Holy Bible, New International Version® (NIV®), Copyright © 1973, 1978, 1984, 2011 by Biblica, Inc.®

Holy Bible, New Living Translation, Copyright © 1996, 2004, 2007 by Tyndale House Publishers, Inc.

The Holy Bible, King James Version, New York: American Bible Society, 1999; Bartleby.com, 2000

## Versions of Scripture in English

(NIV) New International Version

(NLT) New Living Translation

(KJV) King James Version

CPSIA information can be obtained
at www.ICGtesting.com
Printed in the USA
FFOW04n0217080117
31009FF

9 781478 780564